THE GREAT ARC
OF THE WILD SHEEP

THE GREAT ARC
OF THE WILD SHEEP

by

James L. Clark

Foreword by Richard M. Mitchell

SAFARI PRESS, Inc.

OTHER TITLES BY JAMES L. CLARK

Trails of the Hunted (Boston, MA, 1928)
Good Hunting (Norman, OK, 1966)

The frontispiece is an *Ovis poli*, sculptured in bronze by the author. "His fine sturdy body all seems to point to and culminate in support of his massive horns which he always carries with pride and dignity."

–Prince Demidoff

Clark, James L.

ISBN 1-57157-013-6

1994, Long Beach, CA, USA

10 9 8 7 6 5 4 3 2 1

Readers wishing to receive the Safari Press catalog, featuring many fine books on big-game hunting, wingshooting, and firearms, should write the publisher at the address given above.

This is the 53rd book published by Safari Press.

FOREWORD

Although I never met the late James L. Clark, he ranks along with Nikolai M. Przhevalsky and Sven A. Hedin as one of the greatest Western explorer-naturalists to set foot in Central Asia.

Owing to our incomplete knowledge of wild sheep in many parts of the world—especially those in Central Asia—*The Great Arc of the Wild Sheep*, first published in 1964, remains the best treatise on the Old World sheep.

Little has changed in Central Asia since Clark's expeditions in the 1920s. The vast, inhospitable terrain; the political instability of the border areas; the petty, meddlesome bureaucrats; and the remoteness of the game still remain. The greatest difference is that one can now reach Asia from North America within twenty-four hours by air and the distant outposts via jeep. The search for wild sheep, however, still requires arduous treks to the far reaches of the "Roof of the World."

Surprisingly, Argali still remain locally plentiful due to their inaccessible habitat and five thousand years of living in conjunction with local herders and nomads. Since 1980, I have made eight major expeditions to Northwest China and Tibet and have been pleasantly surprised at the abundance of sheep. Today, fledgling conservation and management programs for wild sheep have emerged in China, Mongolia, the former Russian Territories, and Pakistan.

James Clark, explorer and naturalist, carved a niche in Central Asia for later scientists to follow. Thirty years later, his discourse remains unsurpassed, even though since the 1980s forbidden lands have opened their doors to explorers, scientists, and hunters. While Clark laid the cornerstone of knowledge for the Old World sheep, perhaps a new printing of *The Great Arc of the Wild Sheep* will build upon that foundation set down by him some seventy years ago.

RICHARD M. MITCHELL
U.S. Fish and Wildlife Service

Washington, D.C.

PREFACE

This book has come into being through my long-standing interest in and deep respect for the sturdy, power-packed wild sheep.

Although I had hunted and studied many of the North American and Central Asiatic sheep and had through the years sculptured and mounted many complete specimens for The American Museum of Natural History and hundreds of heads at my private studios, I looked upon them mostly from a sculptural standpoint, as creatures of beauty, strength, and character.

My interest in where the sheep came from and in the generic relationship they bore to one another was little more than a casual one. But in recent years my thoughts often wandered back to these magnificent animals and to the glorious mountain countries where I had had my little camps and climbed over rocky crags to hidden basins in search of wild sheep. As with most hunters, "the more I hunted the less I killed." Now I had no further wish to kill; I only desired to know more about these creatures which had so enraptured me.

Beginning with asking pertinent questions of my scientific friends, I found that answers were not always definite or conclusive, and I was referred to a variety of books. Books piled high on my desk. The more I read, the more elusive the answers seemed to be.

Although these wild sheep have been studied and classified and reclassified for well over one hundred years, there still remain many unanswered questions. This is by no means a reflection on those early scientists who have given us a very considerable amount of information. Rather, there have been far too few scientists to cover all the sheep scattered far and wide in the most remote places of the world, where accessibility at best involves substantial expense and months of travel. And once on the scene, the habitats of the sheep are so high and so difficult to negotiate that within the limits of the workable season all too little can be accomplished.

Finding myself faced with a problem that lay like a scattered jigsaw puzzle with some pieces missing, others with frayed and ragged edges, and still others that simply didn't seem to match at all, I delved further into the sheep literature, and as I found pertinent information I outlined a map to show the respective geographical ranges of the sheep. This gave me a comprehensive basic picture of their over-all distribution, and from there on I could plot other information as it unfolded. But the more I read the more confusing it grew, for many of the data were incomplete, contradictory, and inconclusive. My efforts therefore became an interesting challenge—so interesting, in fact, that what I learned as my jigsaw puzzle took form I believe may likewise be of interest to other hunters and laymen, as well as to scientists.

Throughout the text of this book I have endeavored to hold to the minimum the use of taxonomic names, forms, and phrases but in spite of this many are employed, for only by their use can one precisely identify the subject in question. Elsewhere I have used the more or less common or popular terms and names current among sportsmen and laymen.

JAMES L. CLARK

New York City

ACKNOWLEDGMENTS

A<small>LTHOUGH</small> many acknowledgments have been duly recorded throughout this text, there are some that I particularly desire to mention. These are the many institutions and their personnel, state game departments, and individuals who have so graciously and generously responded to my inquiries for specific information and photographs.

It is therefore my pleasure to express special gratitude, to Remington Kellogg, director of the United States National Museum, and David H. Johnson of the same institution for making it possible for me to study their sheep material; John Tee Van, director of the New York Zoological Park, for his permission to study, measure, and photograph many of the heads in their outstanding National Collection of Heads and Horns; Harold T. Green, director of exhibits in the Academy of Natural Sciences of Philadelphia, for permission to study their sheep material and for many photographs shown in this book; the staff of the Department of Mammals of The American Museum of Natural History, particularly George Goodwin and T. Donald Carter, who helped me greatly in selecting the best books from the mass of scientific literature; and the American Geographical Society, New York, for their help in locating and accurately naming many remote geographical areas and places.

Among the individuals to whom I am particularly grateful are my old friend and colleague, the late Roy Chapman Andrews, for his generosity in permitting me to use much of his material and many photographs, and F. Edmond-Blanc, of France, who was not only most generous in his response to my queries concerning the Urials but supplied me with many fine pictures.

Last, but by no means least, I pay homage and thanks to that outstanding British explorer-naturalist, Douglas Carruthers, who without a doubt has had more real field experience with and more knowledge of the Near Eastern and Central Asian sheep than anyone I know. Whenever I wrote to him on questions I was sure he could answer, he replied immediately and generously, offering all help within his power. Needless to say, I have greatly enjoyed and benefited from extensive correspondence with him and from permission to quote from his books and use his photographs.

Photographs not otherwise credited are by the author.

J.L.C.

INTRODUCTION

O F all the coveted big-game trophies of the world there is none more highly prized by ambitious Nimrods than a massive sheep head. To achieve this ambition, the hunter must take to the heights, for such is the habitat of the wild sheep he is seeking.

He may travel to the east or he may turn to the west, but he must hold to mountain country. In a word, he must follow the Great Arc of the Wild Sheep. It is of the Great Arc that I propose to tell: where it spreads and how I came, over a stretch of years and experience, to discover its reality. I have not, of course, traversed the full span of the Great Arc, but it happens that I have been both eyewitness and active participant in sheep-hunting within the two ends of its magnificent and far-reaching curve.

I was an impetuous young man, in my early twenties, when I first touched the North American area of the Great Arc, and, I hope, a more mature hunter when I approached its Asian section many years later. The actual discovery of the Arc concept, however, came only after I had added to my own experiences in the sheep country some degree of knowledge of the sheep lore and literature compiled by others. As I plotted the various habitat localities of the wild sheep on the map, my sculptor's eye was struck by the curving line they formed. Also, I could not help noticing that by a happy coincidence the double curve of the Great Arc bore a strong resemblance to the double curve of the sheep horn. That set me off and I became fascinated with the project of recording the course and character of the wild sheep throughout the world.

A wild sheep is not the biggest or the most dangerous trophy a hunter can bag. But it takes all the wit, skill, stamina, and experience that a man can muster to bring down a really fine head. He is up against the keenest-eyed, wariest, and most cunning of all big game. And never does that mighty sheep stand immobile for those fatal few seconds to look you over, as do many of the other big-game animals. Once a sheep spots you, no matter how far away, he is off and you may never see him again.

Sheep-hunting takes you to the top of the world, where towering mountain peaks sweep on to the horizon and vast valleys plunge thousands of feet below you. He who hunts low will never bag that coveted biggest of big rams.

Those who have never known the fatigue of the grueling climb up rocky crags and over frozen snow fields, the tense impatience of the final stalk, or the nerve-wracking uncertainty of success or failure cannot even begin to realize the toil and torture necessary to attain a good sheep head.

The wisest of the wise, the canniest of all sheep, these old patricians, who have lived their full life and survived its vicissitudes, tuck themselves away in the highest, most inaccessible, hidden basins where only the best of hunters has the will and stamina even to think of going. And once there, the hunter must be on the alert to play the sheep's game, for his quarry is at home in the small labyrinthine sanctuary of crags and canyons which a lifetime of experience has taught him to seek as the most secure and peaceful places to spend the last of his waning years. Here neither man nor beast can enter without the refugee's knowledge, and here it is that, familiar with every nook and cranny, he can slip away into mists or mountains with no one the wiser. Only those who know good "sheep ground" and its telltale signs would stop to seek him out, and only a man with sheep hunter's blood in his veins would linger to spend a bitter-cold night curled up under the shelter of some rock, without food or fire, to brave the chilling winds while he waits for dawn to begin his hunt.

Then with little sleep and numbed limbs he goes forth, slowly and stealthily, like another denizen of the wild to seek his prey. If he plays the game right, he will find his big ram intently feeding and off guard; for never before has he been molested so early. But the hunter is cold—his fingers are too stiff for that slow, delicate trigger-squeeze, should the ram be alerted. In the clear, cold light, distances are deceptive but on he climbs, straining to reach the highest ridge, for never must he let full daylight come with that ram somewhere above him. Now at dawn's coldest hour he wonders if he can stand it, but he dares not make one unnecessary motion—he looks and looks, his eyes blurred with almost frozen teardrops. He casts a second glance below him at a suspicious-looking rock. It *is* his big ram! He waits and ponders. It is a long shot and a difficult one. The head of heads would soon feed out of sight—but should he take the chance? As best he can he draws bead, squeezes the trigger, and fires. The bullet just grazes his sheep's back and spatters on the rock beyond. In one great bound his sheep has disappeared. But he is a real sheep hunter and will try another day—not before another year perhaps, for winter's storms are already closing in. His sheep would be there next fall if the Great Spirit spared him. Feeble perhaps but still with his big head, and it would be far better to take him at that time than leave him to suffer through another bitter winter, only to succumb and have his massive horns buried and lost under the debris of a thundering snowslide.

*   *   *

Many are inclined to think of the wild sheep as just scattered here and there around the world with little reason—but this is not so. A glance at Map 1 in this book will show that although they are rather thinly dispersed, the sheep are confined to a relatively narrow arc of mountain ranges which sweep across three continents. Their preferred habitats are the upper reaches of this almost continuous mountain arc. Nowhere else in the world are true wild sheep to be found, and they are all north of the equator.

Sheep are sturdy, proud, and confident animals. They seem to have confidence only in themselves and are suspicious of everything else. When taking flight they can accomplish unbelievable feats of astuteness in their dash for safety. I have seen a Poli bound down a steep, rock-strewn slope with the speed and grace of a Pronghorn antelope running on the flat.

With powerful binoculars I once watched an American Bighorn

cross a face of rock where his only footing was the single inner toes of his cloven hooves.

There is "sheep ground" and there is "goat ground." In a new hunting area the first thing that a hunter should do is seek out the sheep ground and begin to look for his prey. Sheep grounds are grassy areas that are not too steep. These will be found on the sunny side of the mountains, on the lofty open slopes with near-by outcrops of rocks which provide for a quick getaway in case of a surprise attack. But the best places to look for the really big rams are in the hidden basins high up in the mountains. These are usually in the form of an amphitheater surrounded by rocky walls with an opening at the lower end, through which a small stream drains the area. None of these is too small to overlook, for sheep are often found resting right in the center of them.

Goat ground, on the other hand, is on the rougher, more precipitous slopes, which are also backed by rocky outcrops. Here wild goats find the coarser vegetation which they seem to prefer, leaving the shorter, sweet grass to the sheep.

There is little doubt that our domestic sheep are very remote descendants of one or more of these races of wild sheep. Just when and where their domestication started is not certain, but it is probable that it came to pass somewhere in the Middle East at the western end of the Himalaya and Hindu Kush Mountains, where the Urials, still plentiful today, occasionally range and breed with the domestic stock.

Weighing from a minimum of 150 pounds in the Mediterranean and Near Eastern areas to a maximum of 400 to 450 pounds in Central Asia, the wild sheep are sturdily built, with powerful rumps and deep withers strongly muscled to take up the shock when landing on their front feet and also to carry their heavy horns. Quiet, peace-loving animals, they bother no one and want to be left alone. But if they must fight, they are a vicious and telling foe.

Sheep will live to the age of about fifteen years, but they seldom attain that age because of hunters or being winter-killed when caught in snowslides or in heavy snows, when they fall prey to predators or starvation. Their greatest enemy is the wolf, who either runs them down or finds them helpless in deep snow. In spring the eagles and possibly the larger carnivores, such as the snow leopard or mountain lion take the young.

Although the sheep prefer the grass of the upland meadows, they will also take to roots and other forms of vegetation not of their normal diet. Early one morning in the month of May when hunting *Ovis poli* in Central Asia, I observed a good ram in the middle of an arid, sandy valley apparently pawing for some sort of food with his front feet. Curious to learn what he was after, I made a careful stalk and dropped him in his tracks. Digging into one of the shallow holes he had made, I found the green, nibbled tops of a bulbous plant that had not yet broken through the surface. By looks and taste it proved to be a wild onion, and a very strong one too. Now I knew what gave these sheep the very pungent odor I had sensed when skinning them and also gave the same unsavory flavor to their meat. Apparently these wild onions were the first green food to be had in the spring.

Although sheep will move back and forth from their summer and winter ranges, they do not migrate. Born to live their lives within a relatively small radius of but a few miles, they learn to know every foot of ground where they can elude their enemy.

Only through the centuries do they "drift" rather than "migrate" to new lands, forced perhaps by overcrowded pasture, fire, or extended droughts, which have left their ground denuded.

So persistently will they adhere to the region of their birth that they will be all but wiped out by their enemies before they will take up new ground. Sheep have been observed crossing desert stretches going from one mountain range to another, but this also may be caused by conditions unfavorable to survival, and it is not certain that they do not return to their place of origin as conditions require or permit.

Although sheep are thought of as mountain animals, and rightly so, they will under duress take to lower ground. There are now places along their Great Arc where they may be seen from salt water, and the American Desert sheep have been observed in areas known to be below sea level.

xvii

Horns of Wild Sheep

Since the horns of wild sheep are their dominating feature, it seems appropriate that we emphasize their growth, conformation, structure, and resulting characteristics as possible factors in their identification, if not their classification. I am inclined to believe that these horn characters are perhaps as stable and reliable as other features used as a basis of classification. Their horns will of course vary somewhat, but so will their other individual characteristics.

A sheep head with one horn removed to show the core
over which the horn grows.

The horns, which grow from the skin like our fingernails, over a conical, bony core, are not shed and are not radically dissimilar, as are those of the antelope and deer tribes. The horns grow to their maximum length in the Poli group of the Russian Pamirs and to the greatest mass and circumference in the Ammon group of Central Asia and Mongolia. Sheep horns attain maturity at about the age of five years, when they will have grown about two-thirds of their over-all length and perhaps 90 per cent of their base circumference. After that it takes twice as long (ten years) to grow the last third.

Yet this shorter section (the last third), of compressed corrugations and year-rings, is all mass and is the all-important feature that endows a head with its coveted bulk and character. The horns begin to get this mass between the third and fourth years, when the horn core begins to bulge along its inner surface as if to reinforce the whole horn-base structure for the vicious battles for supremacy that lie ahead.

It is not uncommon to see sheep horns curling upward on either side of the face, seemingly obstructing the sheep's vision. Nor is it uncommon to see such horns, especially those of old rams, heavily "broomed" at the tips. This brooming, a wearing-away of the horn's tips, which sometimes reduces the horn's length by several inches, was previously believed to be intentional on the part of the sheep. But Ned Frost (of whom more later) told me: "No! Ninety-five percent of brooming resulted from fighting, while the other five percent came from accidents, hitting rocks when feeding or making quick get-aways and from digging for roots with their horns." And Ned added: "Nor do sheep jump off cliffs and land on their horns to break their fall."

All of the more massive, closely curled horns are invariably well broomed, while the lighter, more flaring horns of the Poli group and some of the Urials and the flaring horns of the Dall sheep, both black and white, are seldom broomed. This may be because these flaring heads do not make good fighting weapons, while the massive, closely curled horns do. I doubt if the temperaments of different sheep vary enough to make one group fighters and another group pacifists. I believe that they all fight, but those with the flaring horns are perhaps less prone to do so when they find their horns awkward and ineffective.

Some sheep heads carry a recognizable difference in the facial angle at which the horns rise from the skull. This is particularly noticeable in the Poli and its nearest relatives (sometimes called the "Poli family") and in the Mouflon (*Ovis musimon*). Believing this character to be basic in skull structure and not an individual variation, I have arbitrarily divided the sheep into two groups, shown as A and B in the drawings below:

A    B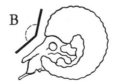

In thus analyzing the sheep we find the "low-brows" and "high-brows" to be as follows:

A—Low-brows	B—High-brows
Ovis musimon (Mouflon)	All Urials
Ovis ammon severtzovi	*Ovis ammon sairensis*
Ovis ammon nigrimontana	*Ovis ammon ammon*
Ovis ammon poli	*Ovis ammon hodgsoni*
Ovis ammon humei	*Ovis ammon darwini*
Ovis ammon karelini	*Ovis nivicola*
Ovis ammon littledalei	*Ovis dalli*
	Ovis canadensis

If this feature holds constant, as now appears, it would at least be a first step in segregating heads that now carry no identifying data.

A powerful lot of energy goes into the growing of these huge horns, and their corrugations reflect this in the amount of horn material deposited during the months of abundant grazing. Like "tree-rings," the corrugations reflect these intake-and-rest periods and also show, in the horn's "year-rings," the two or more dormant months of winter when the food supply is very lean and the sheep subsist almost entirely on their stored-up fat. Between the horn's year-rings are approximately ten heavier corrugations. These reflect the months of plenty. Growth is greatest in midsummer, when the grazing is at its best and with clear weather and the light of the summer moon the sheep can feed throughout the night. Unevenness or definite interruptions in these corrugations are indications of sicknesses, droughts, or other disruptions in their feeding habits.

Curious to know just how heavy a "heavy" sheep head is, I made some tests with scales, all heads (horns and skull, without lower jaws) being fully adult and thoroughly dried. They are as follows: the Argalis of Central Asia (the largest of all sheep), 49 pounds; the American Bighorns (the largest North American sheep), 40 pounds; the Marco Polo sheep (the longest-horned sheep), 25 pounds; and the Kamchatka Bighorns (the sheep of eastern Siberia), 15 pounds.

Because of the wide variance in the size and weight of horns available in the Moufloniforme group (the smallest of sheep from the Near Eastern countries), I could find no head to serve as a fair basis for comparison. But as they are generally lighter and more slender in horn growth, I believe that they would run considerably less in weight than the somewhat heavier Kamchatka Bighorns, perhaps in the vicinity of plus-or-minus ten pounds, with most of them under rather than over this figure.

Horn Sections

In sheep literature the descriptions of sheep horns are so difficult to visualize that I resorted to taking various horn sections to help me better to understand them, so that I could more adequately impart their characteristic forms to my readers. Although the results were not all that I had expected, they brought to light some interesting facts concerning the true shape of horns.

So that a just comparison could be made, the sections were all taken at the five-year ring of the right horn, when the horns were all but fully matured. Some of these horn sections will be seen in Appendix VIII.

Broken Poli Horns

In the Russian Pamirs, I was interested in the many Poli heads with a single broken horn. These breaks were observed both on the living animals and among the old heads lying around the Kirghiz abandoned encampments. Never were both horns broken, and this

A Poli horn broken in combat

single break invariably occurred at about the end of the horn core. Sometimes, however, it was even closer to the head.

Rarely did Poli horns show any shattering at the tips, and then only minor ones. Having seen no other sheep with horns so broken, I think that this must be the result of the great leverage exerted on this particular part of the horn when the long horns are perhaps struck a powerful, glancing blow in fighting.

It seems incredible that such tough and strong materials as comprise these horns could be so broken by the mere impact of the sheep's body thrust. But as this could only happen in fighting, it shows with what extraordinary power and impact two fighting sheep must meet.

This broken-horn condition was frequent enough to cause me to look twice before taking a big Poli as a specimen.

How to Tell the Age of a Sheep

The age of a sheep may be quite accurately determined by the year-rings of his horns. These appear as definite lines encircling the horns, marking the period of arrested growth during the lean winter months. During the first three or four years these rings are several inches apart, but thereafter they grow progressively closer, sometimes becoming so confused with normal corrugation as to make their identification quite difficult. When this is the case one

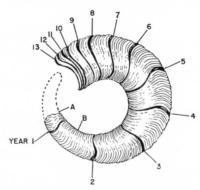

must arbitrarily establish these later yearly ring spacings (as indicated in the above drawing by the numbers 10, 11, 12, and 13), which would thereby show this particular head to be thirteen years old).

When a horn is broomed one must estimate how much of the tip is missing. If broomed off to A in the above drawing, the small circumference of the horn at this point and the presence of the first year-ring (one year) would indicate that three-quarters of a year's growth had been lost. If broomed off as far as B, then the larger circumference at this point and the very considerable weight of the horn at the nearest year-ring would indicate that a full year and a half had been lost. Then beginning with first year-ring, or where it should be, and counting this as year one, you may continue toward the base, adding one year for each ring.

Although there is considerable individual variation in horn spread and in horn-beam divergence, some of the sheep groups will reflect a tendency to hold closely to one of the three basic types illustrated below.

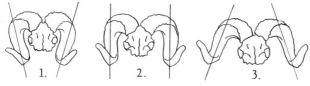

1, Converging; 2, Parallel; 3, Diverging

Scientists separate the wild sheep into two general groups, the "round" horns and the "triangular" horns, but this is not easily accomplished. All sheep horns, round or triangular, are basically triangular (scalene) during the first two or three years of their growth. After that the horns begin to swell or bulge at their base, gradually losing this thin, flat-sided shape. The horns of the Moufloniformes alone seem to retain the triangular shape, but the older they grow, the more lopsided the triangle becomes. In the larger, more massive round-horned group, although they swell to bulge laterally, they are neither round nor triangular, and one must stretch his imagination considerably if he ventures to say which a horn is. Frankly, I find difficulty in so dividing them.

Color and Color-Patterns of Wild Sheep

Present in all wild sheep is a more or less basic color-pattern. This is made up of an over-all body-color, white muzzle and under-chin, white under parts, a white rump-patch, and white edgings running down the rear of all four legs. There is also a darkish band running along the sides of the body from the elbows to the flanks, dividing the upper and under body-colors.

Although this pattern is not present in the Alaskan White sheep because of its being all white, most of it is present in its cousin, the Stone sheep, and permanently so in the Mouflon, the latter carrying in addition saddle- and flank-patches of white and nearly all-white lower legs.

The sheep's over-all basic color ranges from a very dark, almost blackish chestnut-brown, as in the Mouflons, through lighter shades of chestnut into darker, then lighter buffs, as in some of the lighter-colored Urials and Desert Bighorns.

All these colors and shades will vary somewhat within the different species and subspecies, but with the exception of the White Dall sheep they are the foundation of a sheep's coloring. And there are other factors that give variance to a sheep's pelage, such as age, sex, the seasonal changes of fresh new coats in spring and fall, the wearing-away of the hair tips, fading, the lighting under which they are observed, and of course individual color variation. Therefore, whatever the color or color-pattern of a sheep may be, it persists within these limits, and we may keep this in mind to help us better to understand some rather confusing descriptions. Color cannot be accurately described in a few simple words, and when embellished it becomes all the more confusing. Thus it is that a chestnut-brown can go into varying shades of reds and from reds into lighter buffs.

Therefore the reader may find my interpretation of colors as unsatisfactory as I have sometimes found them in the sheep literature; if so, he will have to make the best guess he can to please his own color palette. The white bibs and neck- or throat-ruffs are confined to the Argali and Moufloniforme groups alone.

The color of sheep horns also varies, but within a given group or species the color remains about the same. Basically most horns are a light dirty-ocher, but if a sheep's pelage is dark, the horns growing from the skin will reflect a somewhat darker coloration, while an overtone tinge may be added from vegetable saps and the dust of the soil.

The Groups of Wild Sheep

The wild sheep of the world may be divided into five general groups: Moufloniformes of the Mediterranean Islands and Middle Eastern countries, Argalis or Ammons of Central Asia, Asiatic Bighorns of Eastern Siberia, Dallis of Alaska and Northern British Columbia, and North American Bighorns of western North America.

The maps in this book will show the general distribution of these sheep and the Great Arc of mountainous country to which they are confined. To plot their habitats more accurately would involve much research and then not be conclusive, for there is much that is yet to be determined, particularly concerning the sheep of central and eastern Asia.

Measurements and weights I have taken from various sources, and unless so specified they cannot be assumed to mean maximum, minimum, or even average. Scientific names, although the simplest and most positive method of precisely identifying an animal, can be confusing to one unfamiliar with them, and a clarification of them may be helpful. All true sheep are given the generic name *Ovis*. The second name is that of the species, or particular kind of *Ovis*, such as *Ovis ammon*. The third name is the subspecies, or one of the variations of that particular species of *ammon*. Thus we have *Ovis ammon poli*, *poli* being one particular kind of *ammon* in the over-all *Ovis ammon* group. When the second name is repeated, as in *Ovis ammon ammon*, this means that this particular sheep is the master species or type, the first of the species to be authoritatively described and named. As other sheep are found carrying variations, almost but not exactly like the type specimen, they are described and given a distinguishing third name, which identifies them as another particular variant of the master species, such as *Ovis am-*

mon hodgsoni. And so it is that we may have several subspecies, the generic name only being written with a capital letter.

Not infrequently such zoological groupings are reshuffled. This occurs when some scientist, having obtained fuller or more concrete data regarding some individual specimen or specimens, feels justified in reclassifying their position. During this process some subspecies and even species may be eliminated entirely or new ones may be added. The scientist then has the privilege of renaming the new species or subspecies and selecting the proper nomenclature to make its classification clear. Thus it is that in our listing the "recognized" sheep of today may not be the "recognized" sheep of tomorrow.

Letter Codes Used for the Simplification of the Text

Because there will be much repetition of data on the pages that follow, I have tried to simplify the text by using the following letter codes:

A.M.N.H.	The American Museum of Natural History, New York City.
H.B.C.	Horn-base circumference; circumference around base of largest horn.
H.C.D.	Horn-circle diameter, as determined by horn curl; taken across one horn from outer edges.
H.L.	Horn length; length of longest horn, from base to tip, over outer curl.
H.S.	Horn spread; distance from outer edge of horn's beam at widest point, taken when tips are less.
H.T.	Horn-tip spread; distance between outer edges of horn tips.
L.H.	Left horn.
N.C.H.H.	National Collection of Heads and Horns at the N.Y.Z.P.
N.Y.Z.P.	New York Zoological Park, New York City.
R.H.	Right horn.
S.H.	Shoulder height; height of animal at shoulders.
Sk. L.	Skull length; over-all length of skull, from premaxillary to occipital.
Wt.	Weight—as given; but not verified, unless so stated.

My First Trip into Sheep Country

My first experience with wild sheep came a few years after I had been chosen from the modeling class of the Rhode Island School of Design as a young sculptor who could put life into "stuffed" animals by modeling their beautiful forms in clay rather than in crude excelsior. Thus at the age of eighteen I entered The American Museum of Natural History, in New York City, to start my career as an artist with little thought that I would drift into taxidermy. But this came about easily, for I had a natural flair for mechanics as well as for art and a love of the out-of-doors, and I soon became deeply interested in the animals I was sculpturing and in the technique of preparing and applying their skins to my final model. Of course I went to the zoos to study, photograph, and model, getting up in the longer summer days as soon as daylight came, then working in a zoo until eight, when I would go somewhere for breakfast, and be in the Museum studios at nine.

My love of animals and the out-of-doors came to me, I believe, from my maternal grandfather, a Forty-niner, who rounded Cape Horn on an eleven-month voyage in a small sailing ship to dig gold in California. I was always fascinated when my mother, who was also a lover of nature, would relate the many details of Grandfather's trip, especially how he came back by way of the Isthmus of Panama carried in a chair lashed to the back of an Indian with a tumpline across his forehead.

It was when I began to feel the need of seeing wild animals in their native habitat, subconsciously graduating from the rather forlorn zoo specimens of those days to a keen awareness of the beauty in animals, especially the beauty of wild animals, that I somewhat hesitantly put my case to Herman C. Bumpus, then director of the Museum, and the very man who had initiated my coming to that wonderful institution. When I told him how keenly I felt this need to improve my work, he was heartily in accord and suggested that I go to Yellowstone Park, where I could observe the greatest variety of American big game under the most favorable conditions.

This suggestion exceeded my fondest dreams. I was happy beyond words to think that I was going to such a wonderful place. Still, after all, it was a family tradition, for I was going west as my grandfather had, on a great adventure. However, while my dear old granddad returned with only a few gold nuggets, I came back with a wealth of knowledge of how beautiful and healthy wild animals really looked and how they should look when mounted.

I was awed by the challenge to make them so. Could I rise to meet that challenge? I am still trying!

It was a lucky chance that brought me, a young and green tenderfoot from the East, into the camp of Ned Frost near Cody, Wyoming, for my first sheep hunt. Ned's older brother happened to be one of Cody's picturesque gambling-saloon keepers of those early days in the West, an upstanding, fine fellow of the type familiar to us in the movies nowadays, and in his resort I got a firsthand impression of cowboys in chaps and buckskins, ready to shoot from the hip without notice. Ned, however, was a man of different tastes and talents; he loved big game and the joy of hunting and became one of Wyoming's great sheep hunters. It was from Ned that I acquired real insight into the tricks and mysteries of sheep and sheep-hunting.

Under Ned's guiding hand, I made my way into Yellowstone Park for my first experience with wild sheep. There I spent hours watching bands of sheep through my glasses. Although protected, they were by no means tame and I could not get very close to them. But it was thrilling even to see sheep, as well as other wildlife. Of all the big-game animals I have studied and collected, I have always found the sheep by far the most interesting. Being rather nervous and high-strung creatures, they are rarely found in zoos, and I had never before had the opportunity of seeing one alive.

When leaving the Park, Ned took me into the outlying hunting country, where with a bona fide hunting license I collected and studied the Pronghorn antelope, elk, deer, and sheep. This was just what I had come for—a close-up analysis of the animals' fine, rounded bodies and the many detailed forms of their beautiful heads, and the coloring of their eyes, nostrils, lips, and even their tongues. Equally important to me was the opportunity to study and sketch their muscular and skeletal anatomy after their skins had been carefully removed and cared for as Museum specimens. Such data would give me the very fundamentals for the clay models which I would later have to sculpture for the taxidermists.

Thus it was that this new experience whetted an insatiable desire to go to the field for more and more such firsthand knowledge. During the years that followed I made many expeditions to the Canadian North Woods, Alaska, British Columbia, Alberta, and the big-game fields of our West, not to mention Africa, Central Asia, and Indochina, spending even more time watching and studying game through my glasses than hunting it. This was important, for in setting up the habitat groups for the Museum I had to know as much about each animal's habits and native haunts as I did about his anatomy. Both had to be correct.

And now let us see what these various sheep are, what they look like, and where they are to be found. Let us follow the Great Arc.

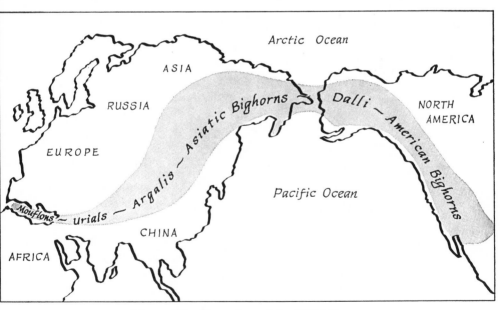

Map 1. The Great Arc of the Wild Sheep.

CONTENTS

xxxi

ILLUSTRATIONS

MAPS

PART ONE

*The Sheep of the Mediterranean Islands
and the Near-Eastern Countries*

THE Great Arc of the Wild Sheep begins with the little Mouflons at the western end of the Mediterranean, where they inhabit the islands of Corsica and Sardinia. From there the arc sweeps eastward through Asia Minor, Central Asia, and Siberia to cross the Bering Sea into North America, where it follows the Rocky Mountains southward to Old Mexico—always, it will be remembered, north of the equator.

Elsewhere in the world one would look in vain for the wild sheep.

THE MOUFLONS

Ovis musimon

The Mouflon (*Ovis musimon*)

THE MOUFLON is by far the best-dressed of all the Moufloniformes, if not the best-dressed of all the wild sheep of the world. With his rich, chestnut-brown coat and splashes of white, tawny-yellow, and black he is a spectacular little fellow. It seems as though he served as a gentlemanly European model for his Asiatic kin, for one observes a similar elegance of style and coloration among the several species of Urials ranging most of the Near Eastern countries.

The true Mouflon, the species type and the lone representative of this species *musimon*, is now confined to the islands of Corsica and Sardinia. It once ranged farther eastward through the Grecian Islands as far as Cyprus. Those found in Europe today were never indigenous there, but are transplants brought in from these islands.

The Mouflon is a sturdy little sheep, about 27 inches at the shoulders and weighing around 150 pounds. In full winter coat he carries a heavy throat-ruff of white, tan, and black, a more or less characteristic feature of the Urial group, which we will shortly discuss. His horns are rather long, rounded, and slender. In base circumference they will measure up to 10 inches and are considerably more rounded in beam than those of the Urial.

The nine-and-one-half-year-old ram, pictured above, in the N.C.H.H. of the N.Y.Z.P., is an exceptionally good ram with horn measurements as follows: H.L. 32"; H.B.C. 8¾"; H.T. 14¾"; while the maximum spread of the horns beams are 18¼".

In the younger Mouflon rams, their horns follow a flat plane which carries their horn-tips in toward the neck.

They range the high, broken mountain tops of Corsica and Sardinia at an elevation of about six thousand feet where a thick cover, of a type of heather, some six feet or more in height, gives them shelter and protection. Grassy glades interspersed where they come to feed at dawn and dusk give them good grazing. This high heather-cover has perhaps, more than any other factor, saved them from extinction for it is most difficult for an enemy to enter. And here, if they are pursued, the Mouflons can easily elude their enemies.

The Mouflon and the Urial of Cyprus are the only two sheep whose habitat encompasses forested areas. But this is not by choice, for sheep are inherently fearful of any bush or tree where an enemy may lurk. Rather, they have no alternative, for being on islands, they have no other place to go.

THE URIALS

The Punjab Urial (*Ovis vignei punjabiensis*). This fine Punjab Urial picture gives a good idea of what most of the Urials look like. It shows the general conformation, swept-back horns, and throat- and brisket-ruffs, which are the dominating features of these interesting little sheep.

Horns will deviate somewhat with individual and group variations, and the character of the neck-ruff will change in both prominence and color, but it will serve the reader well to keep this picture in mind as we discuss the Urial's several races.

GENERALLY SPEAKING, the Urials are a low-altitude sheep, ranging under ten thousand feet, while the Argalis are a high-altitude sheep, ranging above that height.[1] Thus there is neither conflict nor inter-

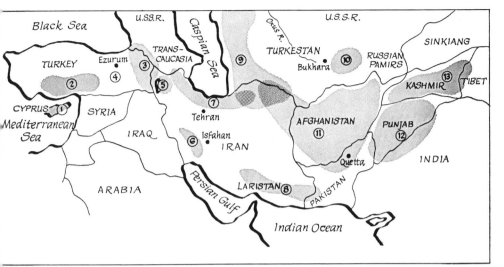

Map 2. Distribution Map of the Urials. 1, *Ovis ophion ophion*; 2, *Ovis ophion anatolica*; 3, *Ovis ophion armeniana*; 4, *Ovis gmelini gmelini*; 5, *Ovis gmelini urmiana*; 6, *Ovis gmelini isphahanica*; 7, *Ovis orientalis*; 8, *Ovis laristan*; 9, *Ovis vignei arkal*; 10, *Ovis vignei bochariensis*; 11, *Ovis vignei cycloceros*; 12, *Ovis vignei punjabiensis*; 13, *Ovis vignei vignei*.

gradation between them. As a rule the Urials follow the river valleys, where they range on the flanking promontories rising sharply between adjoining tributaries. These offer ample grazing while being rough enough to provide them with a quick getaway. They do not hesitate to descend to lower ground to graze or drink when undisturbed. And when their habitat is in lower hills bordering arid, desertlike country they are sometimes to be found in some of the outlying, detached, rocky uplifts of these areas.

In size they run from about twenty-six to thirty-three inches at the shoulders. Although the backward thrust and swing-in of the horn's tips are strong features, more prominent perhaps is the large neck-ruff. This begins as a long fringe starting on the rear half of each cheek, comes together and blends into a narrow, wavy mane running down the front of the neck, and terminates in a very conspicuous, projecting brisket-ruff.

Although the neck-ruff varies in prominence and color-pattern

[1] For the classification listing of the Mouflon and Urial group, see Appendix II.

7

within this large group, it is to be found more or less developed on all Urials and is at its best in the higher country of northern India.

At the eastern end of their range the Urials are confronted with the ever-rising buttresses of the Hindu Kush and western Himalayas. Then, keeping to lower ground and river valleys, they fan out, some going southward into Pakistan and the river valleys of northern India, and others turning northward into the more arid, desertlike areas of southern Russian Turkestan. There some of them become almost desert dwellers, living their lives in the low, dry foothills skirting these deserts.

The Urials of Cyprus and the Near Eastern Countries

Although Moufloniformes is perhaps a more proper name for these species of sheep, which range the Near Eastern countries, for simplicity's sake I choose to use a name more commonly applied— "Urial" or "Urials" (sometimes spelled "Oorial) to designate any one or all of these smaller Asiatic sheep. The Mouflons and Urials are very closely related but scientists have separated them, leaving the Mouflon as a single, distinct species, while dividing the Urials into six species and eight subspecies.

While the darker, more vividly colored Mouflon carries a rounder, curling horn, the basic color-pattern, heavy neck-ruff, and general conformation are typically Urial. But as one moves eastward, the Urials gradually become larger, somewhat less marked in color and color-pattern, and generally more reddish in over-all coloration, from which they get the name of "Red" Rams. However, as they near the eastern end of their range, there is a tendency to lose much of this red to an overtone of gray.

The horns also change somewhat, growing longer and heavier, becoming more triangular and more heavily corrugated, with a strong tendency toward a backward sweep of the tips, which at times terminate very close to the back of the neck.

The Urials are the only group of sheep whose horns do not consistently carry the basic horn growth of a forward spiral. While some of them definitely do spiral, many others, even in the same race, do not.

Nor does any one race of Urial consistently appear to carry any one of these phases of horn growth. We may someday find from a large series of horns that some of these Urial races are more prone to one phase of this horn variation than to another. But at present their horn formations offer little help as indices of their particular race. Some believe that these deviations from the usual forward spiral are abnormalities, but if this is true, the abnormalities appear to be quite prevalent.

The Cyprus Urial

Ovis ophion ophion

After the photo by R. R. Waterer

ON THE ISLAND of Cyprus, lying about one hundred miles off the southern coast of Turkey, we come to our first true Urial. Sometimes called the Cyprus Mouflon, Cyprus wild sheep, or Cyprus Red Ram, it is said to be the smallest and most primitive of all the Urial group, with a shoulder height of about 25 or 26 inches. Measurements given for one set of horns are: H.L. 24″; H.T. 4½″. The horn-base circumference seldom exceeds 8 inches. Although there is some variance in the horn growth, the horns swing backward and inward well toward the nape of the neck, often terminating with the tips but a few inches apart.

Ranging the Paphos Forests of the six- to seven-thousand-foot Troodos Mountains of central Cyprus, their color and color-pattern are similar to those of the Mouflon but somewhat less vivid. They carry a smaller throat-ruff and only a slight suggestion of saddle-patch. Their main difference from the Mouflon lies in the horn growth, for these sheep carry the swept-back horns common to the Urials instead of the forward-spiraling horns common to the Mouflons.

R. R. Waterer, who until recently was conservator of forests in Cyprus and did much to protect these little sheep from extinction, wrote in the *Journal* of the Society for the Preservation of the Fauna of the [British] Empire (November, 1949):

"These sheep (*O. o. ophion*) are one of the few [Urials] who like a forest habitat but this is perhaps because living on the forest-covered Isle of Cyprus there is no other choice. Their habitat is similar to that of the true Mouflon of Corsica, being rugged hills nearly covered with thick forests.

"In the wild state Mouflons [the Cyprus Mouflon or Urial] are extremely shy, agile, swift in movement and therefore difficult to approach. The territory in which they live is steep mountain land covered with forest growth, much of which is a dense evergreen dwarf-oak. A mature male Mouflon [Urial] is a powerful, well-built and handsome animal. The winter coat is a heavy and dense dull-brown hair, with a conspicuous light-grey saddle across the withers and black throat-mane. The summer coat is short and sleek, of an even brown color with white underparts. The horns are heavy and sickle-shaped."

It is interesting to note that Mr. Waterer refers to the Cyprus Urials as "Mouflon," which is an indication of how a Britisher feels about their similarity.

From here on to the eastern end of their range the Urials inhabit country that, although often rising to ten thousand feet or more, is arid and hot and for the most part carries a ground-cover that is semi-desertlike in character.

The Anatolian Urial
Ovis ophion anatolica

ON THE MAINLAND of Turkey just north of the island of Cyprus we come to our first mainland Urial, ranging in the coastal Bolkar Mountains of Asia Minor. They are said to inhabit also the near-by southern slopes of the Taurus and the Ala Dag Mountain district of Eregli, ranging eastward through south-central Turkey for an undetermined distance.

Although I have been unable to locate either a specimen or a photograph of this particular sheep, I believe that we may assume them to be more like the following mainland Urials than those of Cyprus or Corsica, with the data on one specimen as follows: S.H. 33″; H.L. 24–40″; H.B.C. 8–10″; and the convergence of the horn tips, which is decidedly variable, running from 5½ to 17″.

From the above shoulder height of 33 inches, as against that of the Cyprus Urial of 26 inches, a difference of 7 inches, it is evident that *anatolica* is a considerably larger animal. However, with only one set of measurements for each race, we must accept these with reservation, for only by measuring several individuals from each group and getting an average on each could a fair and reliable comparison be attained. However, from here on, it will be noted that the Urials all run somewhat larger in body and horn.

As to color, their somewhat lighter-reddish coat takes on a tinge of ocher, which persists in the rest of the Urials as well. Their neck-ruff also lightens somewhat and the saddle-patch begins to weaken. As with most animals, the winter coat is darker, richer, and more vivid in coloration and pattern, while in summer it changes to lighter tones, with the markings far less conspicuous.

The Armenian Urial

Ovis ophion armeniana

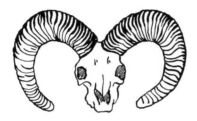

MOVING EASTWARD along the Great Arc, we pick up our next Urial along the northeastern border of Turkey where it joins the Russian and Iranian countries. Here are Mount Ararat, Armenia, Transcaucasia, and, some three hundred miles beyond, the Caspian Sea. From here on until the end of their range in northeastern India the Urial chain is practically unbroken.

There is little in literature regarding this Urial, except very brief scientific descriptions. Apparently this particular Urial has been little hunted by Western sportsmen, who as a rule bring back much practical information to give to us in their hunting books and magazine articles.

Although many of the locality names given are difficult and even sometimes impossible to find on the maps, the range of this Urial is along the high, mountainous borders of northeastern Turkey, Armenia, and Iran and as far south as Lake Urmia.

The *Ovis ophion armeniana* are reported as graceful sheep with yellowish-brown body coats and displaying well-defined saddle-patches. During the winter months they carry a well-developed, dark-brown throat-ruff. Their horns follow the usual flattened plane with about a three-quarter curl and converging terminal tips. Measurements given for one of these Urials run: S.H. 33″; H.L. 40½″ (max.); H.B.C. 10½″; H.T. 5½″. These figures reflect a good-sized animal with a very creditable horn growth.

13

The Erzerum Urial

Ovis gmelini gmelini

THIS IS A MYSTERY URIAL, which persistently lingers in the literature as a "recognized" species. Yet it is known only by two specimens obtained around the middle of the nineteenth century from the environs of the ancient city of Erzurum (Erzerum) in northeastern Turkey.

When first received by the Zoological Society of London, these specimens were described as "cotypes" from that area, with of course the expectancy that others like them would also be found there. But since then no Urials have ever been seen or reported from that same general area. With the probability that they were brought into Erzurum from afar some scientists have ascribed them to some of the nearest Urials, but as yet no Urial has been found that is exactly like them. With this scanty and indefinite information there is little to be said outside of a quote from Blyth, who described them in 1841:

"Size of an ordinary tame sheep, with a remarkably short coat, of a lively chestnut-fulvous colour, deepest upon the back, the limbs and under parts whitish, with few traces of dark markings, except a finely contrasting black line of more lengthened hair down the front of the neck of the male only, widening to a large patch on the breast; and in both sexes a strip of somewhat lengthened mixed black and white hairs above the mid-joint of the forelimbs anteriorly . . . ; tail small, and very slender; horns of the male subtrigonal, compressed, and very deep, with strongly marked angles and cross-striae, diverging backwards, with a slight arcuation to near the tips, which incline inwards. . . . Horns . . . 20 inches over the curvature. . . . Around the eye and muzzle this species is whitish; the chaffron and front of the limbs are more or less tinged with dusky. . . . Female generally similar, but smaller, with no black down the front of the neck, and in the observed instances hornless."[1]

[1] In Francis Harper, *Extinct and Vanishing Mammals of the Old World*.

14

The Urmian Urial

Ovis gmelini urmiana

NEAR THE LOCALITY of the Armenian Urial, in extreme north-western Iran, lies a large lake called Lake Urmia. In this lake is a sizable island by the name of Koyum Dagh, on which we find *Ovis gmelini urmiana*, a completely isolated race of Urials. Some time after they were discovered and described it was learned that they were never indigenous to the island but had long ago been brought in and established there by some royal prince for his private hunting.

Where they came from no one seems to know or ventures to say. But since the Armenian Urials are their closest neighbors, if only on grounds of accessibility, *armeniana* would appear to be their closest relatives. In spite of the almost unanimous doubt of the validity of *urmiana*'s subspecies classification, it is still carried in sheep literature.

According to Francis Harper, their horns, which measure some twenty inches in length, bend outward without trace of spiral

The Elburz Urial

Ovis orientalis

Courtesy of F. Edmond-Blanc

The Elburz Urial (*Ovis orientalis*). Of this picture, Mr. Edmond-Blanc wrote in a recent letter: "This picture is that of a water-colour painting made by a French specialist after the specimens I had collected and the photos I had taken. Of course that is not very pretty but it is very true. Only the colour [a brownish light-buff] is perhaps a little darker here than it really is. The vegetation and the landscape where the sheep are to be found are just right."

THIS ELBURZ URIAL, represented only by its type species (with no subspecies), is one of the larger races of Urials. Its habitat is the ten-thousand-foot Elburz Mountains of northern Iran encircling the southern end of the Caspian Sea. To the west the Elburz unite with the mountainous country that forms the borderlands between Transcaucasia, Turkey, and northwestern Iran, and here the *orientalis* all but join with the Armenian and Urmian Urials.

16

Until lately another Urial, called *erskinei*, was described as oc-
cupying this western part of the Elburz. But recent opinion considers it impossible for two distinct species to inhabit the same

Courtesy of F. Edmond-Blanc

"The first sheep I shot, which certainly is an *O. orientalis* in spite of
its abnormal spread. . . .—F. Edmond-Blanc

ground without intergradation and the loss of their identities. Accordingly, on the assumption that *erskinei* is the same sheep as
orientalis, *erskinei* has since been reclassified and placed in *orientalis*, which now is the sole inhabitant of this western end of the
Elburz. Measurements given for one *Ovis orientalis* are: S.H. 33";
H.L. 24"; H.B.C. 8".

At the eastern end of these mountains there is however, quite a
different story. Here the Elburz fan out into a series of lesser hills
to cover a large area of eastern Iran, where three other races of
Urial, (*arkal, dolgopolovi*, and *cycloceros*) appear to overlap and
undoubtedly intergrade.

As the eminent French hunter and naturalist, F. Edmond-Blanc,
says: ". . . here, one can never be quite sure what particular sheep
he is getting."

17

Courtesy of F. Edmond-Blanc
Urial habitat of northeastern Iran

I am greatly indebted to Mr. Edmond-Blanc for the several following photographs and comments on *Ovis orientalis*, which he has hunted on two separate occasions. He wrote to me:

"I was always interested in these sheep questions myself, and I had had an opportunity before the war, when I had gone to Russia, to see collections and to have talks with specialists. I was never convinced by their theories, too frequently just founded on the length of horns or of the beard. I even had a mind then to write a book on these animals [Urials] myself, but I gave it up thinking it really too complicated and comparison data quite insufficient." And in another letter: "English names: 'red sheep' or 'gmelin's sheep' and 'Urial' do not correspond to anything nowadays [1957] and are always wrongly used for one or the other of these species.

"I did not weigh them [his Urials] but it is not a very heavy animal; I think it might be 15 English pounds at the utmost. The shoulder height—I did not measure them—I think might be about 30 inches. The month taken [was] September. They showed a pretty good neck-ruff, the colour of it being pale beige, nearly

18

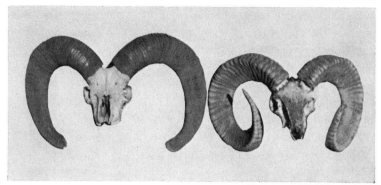

Courtesy of F. Edmond-Blanc

Mr. Edmond-Blanc writes: "This picture distinctly shows the two sub-species of *Ovis orientalis* to be found in the East of Elburz Mountains themselves, as well as in the Khorasson Mountains [near by to the southeast] that, in the East, play the part of the border with Russia, without however being mistaken for the Kopet Dagh Mountains that are in southern Russia [just over the border of northeastern Iran].

"These two specimens, quite different and very typical, were however collected within 100 kilometers from each other and in exactly the same kind of mountains.

"As far as one can know, the right animal seems to be a true *Ovis orientalis orientalis*, Gmelin 1774, and the left one, an *Ovis orientalis erskinei*, Lydekker 1904.

"The female animals of one or of the other of these species which I was able to observe sometimes wore horns and sometimes did not. So I think one must not take this peculiar feature into consideration [as] to class species."

white. Regarding the names *O. o. arkal* and *O. o. cycloceros*. As I told you, all these names do not really mean anything, and it is only with a series of skins, that unfortunately do not exist in any world museum, that one could really make a classification, and I think that for the time being all one can do is just to guess. All I can tell you is, that the sheep [Urials] that have got horns with a close curve are to be found in the East, while those with the big, open spiral are to be found in the West. . . .

"Many of the recognized species and subspecies of Urials are not good [valid] as they all interbreed between themselves when and where they overlap and most of the time it is impossible to know which subspecies one has to deal with."

On this subject Douglas Carruthers wrote in *Unknown Mongolia*: "Many of these Urials are said to mix and breed with the local sheep; difficulty in hunting, due to conflict with domestic sheep and their herdsmen, make them very shy."

The Isfahan Urial

Ovis gmelini isphahanica

MOVING SOUTHWARD in Iran we pick up two rather isolated groups of sheep and then return to our northern Urials to follow them farther eastward to the end of their range.

The first group is the Isfahan Urial, inhabiting the mountains of Pusht Kuh and the Koh-Rud lying some three hundred miles south of Teheran and a little west of the city of Isfahan. These sheep are said to be closely related to those of Lake Urmia, except that their horns are more tightly curled. The second group is the Laristan Urial, which appears to be the most southern of all Urials.

The Laristan Urial

Ovis laristan

LARISTAN is a district or province in extreme south-central Iran, bordering on the Persian Gulf. Here we find this isolated group of *Ovis laristan* Urials, which is represented only by its species type. The limits of its range are not certain, but it is believed to extend eastward into the hill country of southern Pakistan. *Ovis laristan* has even been observed occasionally in the lower areas along the Persian Gulf, where at times the sheep are visible from salt water.

Their shoulder height has been reported at about twenty-eight inches.

As to color, Richard Lydekker said the following in *The Sheep and Its Cousins*: "General color of upper parts in winter dark-brownish yellow; a dark band across the shoulder, with whitish patches before and behind, forming a sort of double saddle-patch; a blackish flank-band; belly white; crown, forehead, and muzzle blackish; a black streak from eye to mouth, and below this a narrower gray one; outer side of ears gray; tail whitish; front and outer side of forelegs above knees, and front of shank below white knees, blackish tawny; elsewhere lower part of forelegs and the whole of lower part of hind legs white; a strong black throat-ruff, with some brownish yellow hairs. In summer the general color changes to chestnut, with almost complete obliteration of the saddle-patch."[1]

This interesting and meticulous color description shows a somewhat varying color-pattern and an undeniably vivid one; incidentally, it illustrates the great value of a good specimen, which Lydekker must have had, in order to describe it thus.

[1] Quoted in Harper, *Extinct and Vanishing Mammals of the Old World*.

The Transcaspian Urial
Ovis vignei arkal

The Transcaspian Urial (*Ovis vignei arkal*). This seven-year-old ram was taken some 150 miles south of the Russian border (far south of its given range) in the Kor-I-Nishpar district of northern Iran. The measurements of the head are as follows: H.L. 38″; H.B.C. 9″; H.T. 23½″.

It is interesting to note in this spiraling head how the horn circle is moved forward to bring the eye back into the center of the circle, rather than behind the horn's tip as is usual with most sheep. If this eye-circle relationship is found to be a constant factor in *arkal*, we may then have a norm helpful to their more positive identification.

The pelage color of this mounted head is a light reddish-buff; face and ears are much the same but lighter; muzzle and under-chin parts are whitish. The throat-ruff is dark with considerable black. A thick cape of long hair tapers down the back of the neck as far as the shoulders. The horns are distinctly corrugated.

RETURNING to our more northern Urials, we find that they suddenly extend their range northward as a great spur into the Ust-Urt Plateau of southern Russia, which borders the eastern shores of the Caspian Sea. This is the northern limit of all Urials, and here they all but rub shoulders with the extreme western end of the Argali group. If there were a connecting link between the two, it might well be here.

I have previously stated that the one characteristic horn-growth feature of the Urial group is the backward sweep of their horns, which swing in at the tips and not forward as with other sheep. While this is generally true, we have a contradiction, for the particular *arkal* horns pictured above definitely turn forward and even spiral. As I have had access to only one specimen of this particular sheep for study, I have no way of knowing whether all *arkal* carry spiraling horns or not. It seems unlikely that such a marked difference in horn growth could be an individual variation; rather it appears to indicate that this whole race must carry spiraling horns.

The only other definitely spiraling Urial head which I have seen is the one shown above in the picture of Edmond-Blanc's two heads, which was taken just to the south of the Arkal range in northern Iran, where these *arkal* overlap the ranges of the more southern Urials carrying the typical, flat-plane, thrust-back horns. Interbreeding could well account for the spiraling horns that occasionally show up in these other overlapped races.

The record horn length for an *arkal*, over curl, is given as 45¼".[1] Lacking shoulder-height measurements, I believe we could assume the *arkal* to stand around 30 to 33 inches at the shoulders.

Its range is given as the hill country of the Ust-Urt Plateau in the southern U.S.S.R., between the Caspian and Aral seas. It is also said to be plentiful in the entire Kopet Dagh country from Tejand to the west end of this range and likewise in the Gurgan (Asterabad) district of northeastern Iran.

Richard Lydekker states in *The Sheep and Its Cousins*: "The arkal sheep of the Ust-Urt Plateau of the Turkoman country, lying to the west of Lake Aral, was described as a distinct species, under the name of *Ovis arkal*, but as it can scarcely be regarded as anything more than a local race of the Urial, it is better known as *O. vignei arkal*. The sheep inhabiting the northern flank of the Elburz Range of Persia and the Kopet Dagh, which divides Persia from Turkestan, do not appear even racially distinct from the *arkal*, although it has been proposed to regard them as representing a distinct race, under the name of *O. v. varentzowi*.

"The *arkal* is specially characterized by the breadth and flatness of the front surface of the horns which has very sharp lateral angles

[1] Rowland Ward, *Records of Big Game*.

and frequently carries very few transverse wrinkles. In old rams, however, the flatness seems to be less marked. These Urial run very large, and the old rams in winter carry long and unusually white throat-ruffs; both these features tending to connect them with the smaller races of the Argali, from which they are not far removed in space."

 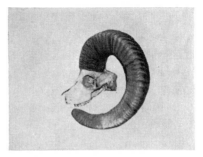

Here we have another *arkal* taken in the same general area as the spiraled head pictured just above. This also is a seven-year-old ram, but it carries little suggestion of a spiral. This could be ascribed to individual variation or intergradation, but it is interesting to note that the horn circle is much more open than that of the mounted head. This open curl is characteristic of the near-by overlapping Afghan Urial, *cycloceros,* ranging from this area to the southwest.

George Goodwin, of The American Museum of Natural History, who collected this specimen in this particular area, gives the following data: "H.L. 35½"; H.B.C. 10½"; H.T. 13½"; [Sk. L. 10½"]; front surface of horns very flat with prominent front angle."

And George Goodwin calls the *arkal* "A bright-colored sheep. Rams with a large white ruff on throat and slender horns which, when fully developed, curve forward below eye; . . . ewes with shorter and straighter horns. Color of males from the upper Gurgan drainage, in November pelage: upperparts uniform ochracheous tawny; sides of face in rams hair-brown mixed with white; a hair-brown lateral stripe broadest behind fore limbs separating the white of underparts from color of back and extending down upper limbs, and in some individuals down lateral side of feet, to hoofs; ankles white or buff."

The Dolgopolovi Urial

Ovis vignei dolgopolovi

I KNOW of no common name for this Urial. Although not isolated in Harper's classification list, because it has been reclassified and placed in *arkal*, *dolgopolovi* frequently turns up in sheep literature as the fourth Urial race inhabiting some of the very same ground in northeastern Iran as *orientalis*, *arkal*, and *cycloceros*. Its type specimen was described from the Russian-Iranian borderland area close to the Caspian Sea, just north of Gurgan. From here it spreads southeastward, adding to the Urial confusion. However, its recent reclassification has helped in some degree to untangle the local Urial picture.

Having no valid features to differentiate *dolgopolovi* from *arkal*, we may assume them to be identical, with the descriptive data on *arkal* serving for both.

The Bukharan Urial
Ovis vignei bochariensis

THE NAME of this Urial stems from Bukhara, a city some 150 miles west of Samarkand on the eastern edge of the Kara-Kum Desert in southern Russian Turkestan. Here the mountain chains of the Tien Shan and the Karakoram meet to taper off in the Hissar Hills, which then disappear in the Kara-Kum and Kyzyl-Kum deserts. Far beyond to the west lies the Caspian Sea and to the south, Afghanistan. The drainages of these high buttresses join to form the Oxus River, which flowing westward and then northward passes the oasis city of Bukhara, emptying eventually into the Sea of Aral.

Believed to be closely related to the Ladak Shapo (*Ovis vignei vignei*) of northern India, *Ovis vignei bochariensis* is also said to be somewhat smaller and with thinner horns. But although it is not the largest of Urials, it is one of the three that range farthest north.

Ovis vignei bochariensis ranges in the upper Zarafshan drainage of the ten-thousand-foot Hissar Mountains to the east of Bukhara, southward to the west of the Poli country of the Russian Pamirs, then westward along the Oxus on the outlying spurs of the Hissar Mountains. It apparently does not go very far north of the Zarafshan, which flows westward to unite with the Oxus at a point one hundred miles or less to the west of Bukhara.

Douglas Carruthers states in *Beyond the Caspian*: "The Oxus has always been considered, and virtually is, the hard and fast dividing-line between the respective zones of these two sections of the genus—the Mouflon [Urials] and the Argali [*ammon*]. Both extend, in various forms, up to the Oxus but neither cross it, nor do they overlap, with the single exception of *Ovis vignei bochariensis*], extending across the Oxus into Eastern Bukhara, but even here there is no overlapping with any form of *ammon*. Further east the Himalayas take on the duty of being the frontier line, and here again there is, in one locality, an overlap, namely, on the

Tibetan-Ladak borderland, where the true *Ovis vignei* actually encroach on the range of the Tibetan *O. ammon.*"

Francis Harper, in *Extinct and Vanishing Mammals of the Old World*, gives its range as: ". . . north to the upper Zarafshan [River], and south to the mountains about the northern tributaries of the Panja [River] (from about Shirabad in the west to Baljuan and Khuljaf in the east)." This area is just north of eastern Afghanistan and west of the Russian Pamirs in southeast Russian Turkestan.

Carruthers further states: "In habits and type of habitat these sheep [Urials] do not seem to differ much from their cousins. They prefer hill country of a type that grants protection by its rugged nature, even if this necessitates living at a low altitude. They seem to prefer steppe vegetation to alpine. In Eastern Bukhara, which has a background of mountains running up to 20,000 ft., the Urial choose for preference the outlying spurs which have an altitude under 10,000 ft. They like the forested hills where pistachio groves flourish on northern slopes. It will be remembered that Marco Polo reported the Urial as being especially numerous hereabouts, actually referring to Hadakstan—'In the mountains are vast numbers of sheep—400, 500, or 600 in a single flock, and all of them wild; and though many of them are taken, they never seem to get aught the scarcer.' That was some years ago, but the Urial are a prolific race and in remote regions such as these they can still muster flocks of a hundred or more during the winter period. . . .

"This Bukharan Urial was first described by Nasonov as a new subspecies, *Ovis vignei bochariensis*, closely allied to *Ovis vignei vignei*, but differing from it by reason of its slightly smaller size, and correspondingly lighter horns. Later on Russian scientists, C. C. Flerov, for instance, in 1935, came to the conclusion that all the various geographical races of Urial, as we know them, were really indistinguishable, that they all intergraded and that they were but an Eastern form of the Persian *Ovis orientalis*. Accordingly, this Urial became, to them, *Ovis vignei* Blyth, or *Ovis orientalis vignei*. Still more recently, however, its position has been clarified, and it is now re-established as *Ovis vignei bochariensis* Nasonov. Doubtless those unexplored mountains just across the Oxus, in northernmost Badakshan, are full of Urial, which we would expect to be *Ovis vignei cycloceros* [the Afghan Urial]."

The Afghan Urial

Ovis vignei cycloceros

HORN MEASUREMENTS of the five-and-one-half-year-old ram shown in the above picture are: H.L. 23″; H.B.C. 9″; H.T. 16″. The skull length of another five-year-old ram measured 10½″.

Ovis vignei cycloceros is thought to be numerically the largest of all the Urial groups, its range covering practically all of Afghanistan and overflowing into the bordering countries of Iran, Russian Turkestan, Pakistan, and the Punjab Province of northern India, as far as the Indus River. The type specimen was described as from Kandagara in southeastern Afghanistan, near the border of Pakistan, not far from Quetta.

Their shoulder height is said to be 32 inches and horn length 41½ inches, which is about the maximum for any Urial. Francis Harper, in *Extinct and Vanishing Mammals of the Old World*, gives the pelage color as follows: "Upper parts uniform yellowish or fawn-colored brown; buttocks, under parts, and inside of limbs white; knees and fore pasterns dirty white; face bluish gray; forepart of forelegs grayish; a black beard, interspersed with white or gray hairs, extending from the jaws to the chest. . . . Horns triangular, strongly wrinkled; curving strongly from the base, forming nearly a circle."

Blanford's Urial

Ovis vignei blanfordi

HERE IS ANOTHER SUBSPECIES of long standing which has also been recently reclassified. Now considered as bearing no valid differences from the Afghan Urial, *cycloceros*, it has been placed in this larger group. First described from the Kelat region of Baluchistan (now Pakistan), it ranges the arid hills in the southern section of this area, where it is locally called "Gad" or "Ghad." Rowland Ward gives the best horn measurements as: H.L. 41½"; H.B.C. 12"; H.T. 15½". These measurements are of the Waziristan head below.

Mr. Warren Page, gun editor of *Field and Stream Magazine*, who hunted this Urial in May, 1957, sent me the following interesting account:

"From Karachi we crossed the Sind Desert to Quetta and headed northwesterly in the direction of Ziarat. About a hundred miles from Quetta we were met by political officers, native chieftains, mule drivers and porters. My expedition was under the aegis of the Pakistan Government [and therefore] directly under the Governor of Baluchistan. In another five hours we came to our hunting camp located in the Pil Range not too far from the Khalifat Mountains. This Pil range runs parallel to the Afghanistan border which lay not far to the west. The country is remarkably like New Mexico in its most rugged areas—between 5,000 and 7,000 feet. Elevation at our camp, however, was 8,500 and we hunted at least as high as 10,500 feet. The easterly slope of this range was relatively gentle, gashed by ravines, more heavily vegetated with assorted types of cactus and shrub trees akin to juniper, and others like piñon and it was on this gentler east slope that 'Gad' were found. The west slope was markhor habitat, a rift of great cliffs shot by nullahs or canyon heads, and extremely precipitous. The biggest horns of the several Gad I secured was 26" around the curl; 28 to 30" being the maximum for this region. The Gads were light in horn, light-colored and not massive, more like a Dall sheep than a Bighorn. Their horns

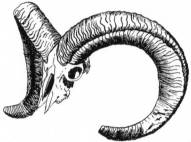

After Lydekker (1913)

A fine Baluchi Urial head. This head was taken in the little northwest province of Waziristan on the border of India between the province of Punjab and Afghanistan. This is about the eastern limit of *cycloceros*, and there is little doubt of its belonging to this race.

Cycloceros are said to carry no saddle-patches and are otherwise so closely related to the Punjab Urial as to be difficult of identification unless the exact locality where specimens are taken is known.

have the characteristic 'shapo' curve, that outward flare and circular curve back in. I did not notice any specific neck or breast markings. The animals were in their summer coat, a grey-brown rock color on the top with some reddish quality showing through, blending to a lighter hair on the belly and general underside. The heaviest Gad of the five I secured weighed at an estimate between 175 and 200 on the hoof, the average being nearer 150 lbs. They ran in bands of three to ten and at this season at least, the old rams seemed to be with the ewes and young, although I glassed one group of four bachelor rams."

The Punjab Urial

Ovis vignei punjabiensis

BEING CLOSE to the border of India, we will move in on that country's Urial, but first we must cross the Indus River. The range of the Punjab Urial is India's northwestern province of Punjab, particularly the area known as the "Salt Range" (hills and/or mountains).

In Punjab this particular sheep is properly called by its native name "Oorial," whereas in near-by Ladakh, where it is practically the same sheep, the natives call it "Shapo."

Measurements given for their horns are: H.L. 37"; H.B.C. 10"; H.T. 7½". One six-year-old ram's skull measured 9¾" in length.

In color it is said to be the reddest of all Urials, with whitish under parts, rump, and lower legs, and with little or no indication of a saddle.

For exactly what this Urial looks like, the reader may turn back to page 6, where he will again see the fine picture of this very sheep.

Courtesy of the New York Zoological Society

An old Urial ram. Probably of the Punjab variety, this specimen is an excellent close-up study for Urial characteristics, showing the neck-ruff, with its three elements: cheek-ruffs, heavy brisket-ruff, and connecting narrow mane down the front of the neck.

Shown also are the darker flank-band running along the side of the body and the whitish lower legs with their black knee-patches and black ankles. The flat plane of the horns' circle, with their backward thrust, is also clearly pictured.

The Shapo or Ladak Urial

Ovis vignei vignei

THE ABOVE six-year-old ram's horns measure as follows: H.L. 31½"; H.B.C. 10¾"; H.S. 26"; H.T. 14½".

The Ladak Urial is listed by Harper as having a horn-length record of 39", a three-quarter horn curl, and standing 38" at the shoulders, which reflects a size equal to that of the Alaskan White sheep.

In India's northernmost province of Kashmir, at the last and most eastern outpost of the Urial group, we find the largest of all Urials in body (if not in horns) and in neck-ruff as well. The Ladak Urial follows the deep valleys of the Indus River system, which fingers it way into the towering Himalayas and over the border into extreme western Tibet. And this is perhaps the only place where two species of wild sheep actually contact and even overlap. Although a Urial and a Tibetan Argali may at times be seen feeding in the same nullah, the Argali being a high-ground animal and the Urial a low-ground sheep, it is only elevation that keeps them apart.

The range of the Ladak Urial is the northern half of Kashmir, from the border of Tibet westward along the southern slopes of the Karakoram to the Hindu Kush. Regarding its distribution Major Gerald Burrard says in his excellent book *Big Game Hunting in the Himalayas and Tibet*: ". . . this handsome sheep [the Ladak Urial] is essentially an inhabitant of the Indus and its river system—not leaving the main stream very far. . . . In the Zaskar Range of Ladak,

35

Shapo and *ammon* often feed in the same nullah near Gya (35 miles south of Leh).... [The Shapo are] more common south of the river [Indus] than north, as far as Chilas.... To the northeast they extend up to the Hindu Kush range beyond Chitral and Gilgit.... Best heads from Punjab Salt Range and Ladak. Horns 30" to 35" found on the more open headlands at the entrance of nullahs."

The above reference to the "Punjab Salt Range" alludes to the area to the southwest where the Punjab Urial is found. As previously noted, many consider the Ladakh and Punjab Urial one and the same sheep, but scientists think differently.

The horn-base circumference is stated to run from 10 to 12½ inches with 11 inches as a high average. Their horn conformation sometimes attains but very seldom exceeds a complete circle. The horn curl follows through on a flat plane, although at times it shows a slight tendency to spiral or flare at the tips. The skull length of four specimens which I measured averaged 9⅜ inches.

The coloring of the Ladak Urial (or Shapo) is said very nearly to approximate that of the *arkal*, to which it is closely related. The light-rufous-brown face carries a white muzzle and a spreading white cheek- or throat-ruff, with a descending, dark neck-fringe terminating in a large, very dark brisket-ruff.

Under parts, lower legs, and rump-patch are whitish. Along the body from elbows to flanks runs a dark band, separating the lighter belly from the upper, somewhat lighter body-color. The neck is reddish-buff, which continues over the body in a somewhat lighter grayish shade. This Urial and the Punjab sheep are the only true wild sheep inhabiting India.

Early one morning when trekking the deep valleys of northern India on my way to the Pamirs, I came upon a group of these Shapos in the valley of the Indus near Gilgit. They had just come down to the river to drink. I quote from my diary: "There were six in all, a fair-sized young ram, three females and two young. Coming on them unexpectedly at about eighty yards as the trail rounded a rocky wall, we saw each other at about the same time and after they took a short, quick look they were off and up the rocks and out of sight in a split second."

"A small sheep, with a reddish-tan, short-haired coat" was my quick analysis. I recall seeing no color-pattern or neck-ruff, but as this canyon country was very hot (in mid-April, at about 4,600 feet), they were evidently in their summer coats, when color-patterns and neck-ruffs would be less conspicuous.

Another experienced sheep hunter, Herbert W. Klein, of Texas, wrote me in August, 1957, as follows: ". . . hunted [the Ladak Urial] at Leh, in eastern Kashmir. Here they call the males 'Sha' or 'Shapo' and the females 'Sham.' We hunted up to 11,000 feet. Estimated weight was 150 lbs. Shoulder height 34". The color was a reddish-tan with white under-chin and belly. Bib not very prominent; throat-ruff dark-brown, almost black. . . . these Kashmir Urials in color look very much like the Armenian red sheep, which we hunted in the Elburz Mountains in northern Iran, inasmuch as they are reddish-tan and some of them do not have any white under their chins at all but have a dark-brown, almost black, semi-beard and then a slight ruff, also black. The real Urial, which Prince Abdorreza shoots in eastern Iran, have white beards and white ruffs, which I understand is very similar to the real Salt Range Urial. He has shot several with horns close to 40 inches, although their horns are long and slender and not massive at the base at all. I saw several in his trophy room at his palace when I was there last October, and my guess is that the base circumference of these heads would only be about 11 or 12½ inches."

PART TWO

The Sheep of Central and Eastern Asia

THE ARGALIS

Ovis ammon

"ARGALI" is the Mongol word for wild sheep or wild ram, but it is now commonly used to designate any one or all of the sheep of the *ammon* group.[1]

There is but one species in this group, *Ovis ammon ammon*, which is the species type; the other eleven divisions are its subspecies. These handsome creatures range the highest mountains of Central Asia. The largest in body and horns of all the wild sheep, they are truly magnificent animals and the finest big-game trophy to fall to the skill of any hunter.

Generally speaking, their main characteristics aside from the size of body are their more triangular, flat-sided, heavily corrugated horns and the large white bib down the front of the neck. Although little noticed in the summer coat, this bib becomes quite conspicuous in full winter pelage. Their coloration is a grayish-tan-buff or fawn on the upper part of the face, neck, and body, with a white muzzle, throat, under parts, and lower legs. The horns are generally light in color, usually being a paler shade of the body-color. Of this group *Ovis ammon hodgsoni*, of Tibet, is stated to be the largest in body, averaging around 48 inches at the shoulders and weighing up to 400 pounds. One *poli* which I collected in the month of May, when it was completely devoid of fat, weighed 234 pounds, but it could well have added another 65 pounds to its weight during the summer and fall to total 300 pounds or more. Although *hodgsoni* is larger and heavier than *poli*, the latter holds the world's record for length of horn over the curl and for horn spread, the record being 75 inches over the curl, with a base circumference of 16 inches and 54½ inches between horn tips. For

[1] For the classification listing of the Argali group, see Appendix III.

over-all massiveness, size, and fine conformation of horns, the Siberian Argali (*Ovis ammon ammon*) tops the list. And just to give their horns more character, they are very heavily corrugated.

Our contact with the Argalis begins immediately as we leave the Urials of southeastern Russian Turkestan and northern India, where these two species of sheep all but overlap. From here the Argalis extend their range eastward through Sinkiang on the north, and then spread out over the lower plateau country of nearly the whole of Mongolia, where they stop just short of the Manchurian border.

Although these Argalis are for the most part the largest of all sheep, the first two we meet (*severtzovi* and *nigrimontana*) are rather small, slightly if at all larger than the near-by Urials. Then come the famous Polis, which are really the start of the larger Argalis, at least from the western end of their over-all limits. From here on they grow even bigger in body and horns and continue so to the eastern limit of their range.

Central Asia is an immense land mass, built on a scale which, like the ocean, makes it appear infinite in its vastness. You may see your objective in the far distance and then march for hours, yet seemingly never come the closer. Some of the mountains are very old and long since eroded into huge, billowy hills showing little rock except in an occasional steeply gashed gully draining these areas. Covered with a nourishing grass and free of trees or bushes, these hills are the habitat of most of these Argali sheep, offering a wide expanse for their all-seeing eyes and a sure and speedy course over undulating ground, where their requirement for speed has developed their longer legs.

This need for agility was vividly brought home to me early one morning in the Tien Shan Mountains where I spotted a band of about ten Littledale rams feeding in a grassy valley about a thousand feet below me. I was watching their lazy ambling when without an instant's warning they suddenly dashed off, fanning out as they headed up the valley. While wondering what had caused their sudden flight, I sighted a pair of wolves just off the heels of the last two. The wolves had almost caught up with them, but the

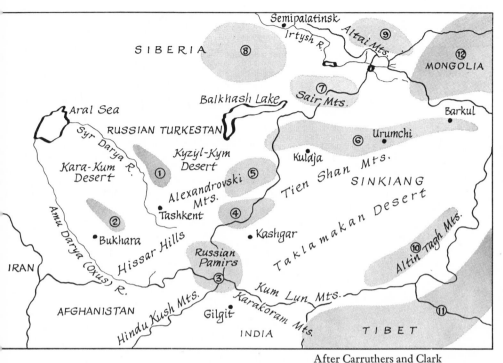

After Carruthers and Clark

Map 3. Distribution Map of the *Ovis ammon*. 1, *Ovis ammon severtzovi*; 2, *Ovis ammon nigrimontana*; 3, *Ovis ammon poli*; 4, *Ovis ammon humei*; 5, *Ovis ammon karelini*; 6, *Ovis ammon littledalei*; 7, *Ovis ammon sairensis*; 8, *Ovis ammon collium*; 9, *Ovis ammon ammon*; 10, *Ovis ammon dalai-lamae*; 11, *Ovis ammon hodgsoni*; 12, *Ovis ammon darwini*.

rams merely put on more speed and it was amazing to see with what apparent ease they left those wolves behind. The wolves soon gave up, to lie down baffled and panting and watch their quarry depart. After some two hundred yards the rams slowed down and with little or no concern resumed their calm grazing. Their strategy of fanning out was obviously to confuse the wolves.

Similar moments of terror dot the days of these creatures of the wild and must be met with instantaneous response if they are to survive. The marvel lies in their astounding equipment of speed plus power, which can be summoned in full force in a split second. Fortunately, by a blessing of nature, there is no lingering memory of fright, and they soon return to their placid grazing as if nothing had happened.

The Severtzov and Bukharan Argali

In the descending arid foothills at the extreme western end of the Himalayas in Russian Turkestan, bordering the large desert areas of Kyzyl-Kum and Kara-Tau, we find two subspecies of small sheep almost rubbing shoulders with the last of the Urial group. Their habitats are similar to those of the near-by Urials, and their size is about the same. But these sheep are of the Argali group, being the westernmost members of the *Ovis ammon* family, which from here extends eastward through Central Asia and Mongolia. Because of their very remote geographical position not much is known about them. Superficially, they appear to resemble the Urials more than the Argalis in both body and horns. But upon close analysis we find their spiraling horns carrying the somewhat larger corrugations of the Argalis. And although their horns are smaller, they are more like the Argalis in character, while the characteristic throat-ruff of the Urials is almost completely missing. In the picture below we now see a suggestion of the Argali "bib."

These sheep are thought by some to be the closest relative to our domestic sheep (*Ovis aries*), and some even believe them to be the very link between the domestic and the wild sheep.

Their habitats are far more arid and desertlike than those of any other members of the Argali group.

44

Severtzov's Argali

Ovis ammon severtzovi

Courtesy of Douglas Carruthers

Severtzov's Argali (*Ovis ammon severtzovi*). This rare and little-known sheep from southwestern Russian Turkestan was taken by Douglas Carruthers, eighty miles northwest of Samarkand, in January, 1908. The man in the picture was Carruthers' native guide.

Carruthers wrote of it as follows: "The horns and skull are in America . . . at the Field Columbian [Chicago] Museum, I think. It is the *only* example of that particular sheep outside of Russia and of great value. Neither we here [in Europe] nor you in America were alive to its value; otherwise one of us ought to have described it and named it after Carruthers. I brought it back in 1908. Nasonov [a Russian scientist] did not name it until 1923!!"

SPECIFICALLY, the range of *Ovis ammon severtzovi* is in the extreme southeastern corner of Russian Turkestan in the Nura-tau

Mountains bordering the Kyzyl-Kum Desert. It is, with the Bukharan Argali, the most western of the Argalis (*Ovis ammon*), whose range extends to the Oxus River, which they are said not to transgress.

As Douglas Carruthers can tell us something about these sheep, I will let him do so, from *Beyond the Caspian*: "Severtzov's sheep is the first of the Argali group to be met with on crossing the Caspian, the intervening region, which embraces the mountains of north-eastern Persia [Iran] and of the Ust Urt plateau [immediately to the north], being occupied by members of the Mouflon [Urial] group, here at the limit of their range northwards. Whether or not there is any intergradation between the two remains to be proved. The head which the late Major Maydon picked up in the Eastern Elburz [mountain range of north-central Iran] (actually at Nardin, half way between Asterabad and Jujurd), which has officially been pronounced to be *severtzovi*, seems to suggest that there is. If so, it is a very interesting discovery, for it is a case of two species overlapping, and one assumes that if there is infiltration, in the case of [wild] sheep, there is a likelihood of interbreeding. But personally I am not satisfied about the classification of this controversial head. It seems improbable that a species would skip a wide area like the Kara Kum Desert, and yet another (mountain) area already occupied by another species, and turn up again beyond them both. Yet the local inhabitants told Maydon that these so-called Bukharan rams came in rarely from the northeast. As for the horns, although they are unlike all others we know of from the Nardin area, and indeed, all other recorded specimens of *Orientalis* and *vignei*, they bear little resemblance to my *severtzovi* from the Kizil Kum, or to those figured by Nasanov in his Monograph. I suggest that they belong to the Moufloniformes [Urials], *not* to the Argaliformes, and that, for the time being, we can safely relegate *severtzovi* to Trans-Oxiana."

There appears to be little difference between the *severtzovi* and the Bukharan Argalis and also between these sheep and the near-by Urials, for they are about the same in size and in horn character. And their habitat is just another near-by section of the same desert-like country.

The Bukharan Argali

Ovis ammon nigrimontana

SOMETIMES CALLED the Turkestan sheep, this small Argali is considered by some to be the same sheep as *severtzovi;* if this is not true, they must be very close relatives. The pictures show an eight-and-one-half-year-old ram in the N.C.H.H., with the following horn measurements: H.L. 36½"; H.B.C. 10¾"; H.T. 24½".

Although the horns are not large, they do reflect the heavier corrugations of the Argali, while the smaller ears are also evidence of their Argali group connection.

Douglas Carruthers describes this sheep as "the smallest, least specialized and most westerly of the *ammon.*" Its range is given as north of the Syr Darya River to part of the southern and southeastern sections of the Kara-Tau and Kyzyl-Kum deserts of extreme southeastern Russian Turkestan. This is just to the south of the range of *severtzovi.* Their color is given as a tan-buff for the body and whitish for the muzzle, neck, under parts, and lower legs.

Marco Polo's Sheep
Ovis ammon poli

Courtesy of the Chicago Natural History Museum

The Marco Polo sheep (*Ovis ammon poli*). From a group in the Chicago Natural History Museum, showing three mature rams, one young ram, and a female, collected by Theodore Roosevelt, Jr., and Kermit Roosevelt near the Russian Pamirs, 1926. This group shows an unusual amount of rocky outcrops and stony ground-cover where sheep would not ordinarily be found because of the lack of grass. They might, however, be en route over a high pass from one valley to another. The reader will note the absence of any "nip-in" of the horns, and the high average of their characteristic flare. This reproduction implies a very dark pelage, which is not the case, but it does show the whitish face and lower limbs. The lighter areas on the neck, shoulder, and flank of the larger ram to the left show the intrusion of lighter hairs that come with age.

OF ALL THE WILD SHEEP of the world, there is none more widely known or better publicized than the Poli. Ever since Marco Polo made his epical journey to the silkened courts of Kublai Khan some seven hundred years ago the world has known of this wild sheep. Marco's reports of this fabulous animal with its extraordinary horns were even beyond the imagination of the learned. And ever since then some reference constantly turns up in current literature to

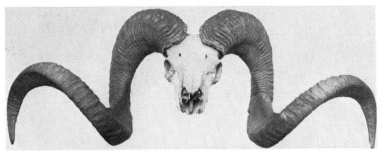

Courtesy of The Academy of Natural Sciences

The Number Two world's record Poli head is reported to have been a "pick-up" in the Yuldaz Valley, Tien Shan Mountains, Sinkiang. Measurements: H.L. 70¾"; H.B.C. 15½"; H.T. 46½". It is presently owned by The Academy of Natural Sciences, Philadelphia.

keep us reminded of this almost mythical animal. It was therefore most logical that when some scientist was to describe and name this sheep, he should immortalize it as the Marco Polo sheep or, in taxonomy, *Ovis poli*. Later, when the classification of all these Central Asian sheep was considered, its name was changed to the present *Ovis ammon poli*.

Douglas Carruthers states in *Beyond the Caspian*: "It is interesting to follow the slow stages by which these great sheep have become known to the West. *Ammon*, first seen and reported in 1253–4 by Father William—the Franciscan Friar of Rubruck in French Flanders—did not receive a name until 1758. *Poli* was recorded, though *not* seen, by Marco Polo in 1273 [he undoubtedly saw some horns], but six centuries elapsed before it was rediscovered by Burnes, in 1834, and the first specimen retrieved by Wood in 1838 enabled Blyth to name it in 1840."

The *poli* range is the Russian Pamirs, in the extreme southeastern corner of Russian Turkestan, and until recently in the adjoining Taghdumbash Mountains to the east, forming the border between northern India and Chinese Turkestan (Sinkiang). *Poli* previously penetrated into northern India as far south as Hunza, but it is doubtful if they could be found there today.

The Morden-Clark Poli Hunt

It was on a chilly spring day of 1925 that *Ovis poli* vividly appeared on my horizon right in the heart of New York City. I was in the Museum studio, absorbed in sculpturing a model for one of our exhibits, my hands gummy with wet clay and, as I later discovered, a patch of the same unflattering material streaked across my chin, when an unexpected caller came up behind me and announced himself as Bill Morden, a friend whom I had not seen for some time.

As he shook my clay-damp hand, he explained that he had come to talk with me about the possibility of my joining him on an expedition into Central Asia, primarily for the purpose of hunting the regal *Ovis poli*. "Go right on with your modeling," he said, "and let me talk you into making the trip with me." I need hardly say that I dropped my modeling tools instantly, wiping away all thought of sculpture and, I hope, the patch of clay on my chin.

Alluring and thrilling as the prospect of a firsthand acquaintance with the great Poli sheep was, we had many an obstacle to overcome before plans could be shaped. In addition to my own personal involvements (wife, private studio, and the Museum), there were first of all the political hurdles to be negotiated. The territory that Bill wanted to penetrate was a very remote and little-known area of Central Asia, which because of its extreme altitude was frequently referred to as "the roof of the world." Here the Great Himalayas seem to stand on end and canyons are breath-takingly deep and precipitous.

The country we proposed hunting was where three great empires meet—India, Russia, and China—with all three ever mutually suspicious lest one get the jump on another and grab off some of these very strategic passes. It was Morden's hope that with the backing of a scientific institution such as The American Museum of Natural History, we might win over at least the Chinese and Indian authorities, for with their age-old reverence for culture and learning these lands would almost surely receive Museum representatives with courtesy. And so indeed it proved, once it had been established that our aims were along the lines of study and collecting for scientific purposes, for we were not only to gather information and specimens of *Ovis poli* but to assemble collections and data on other wildlife of the region. Moreover, this area was so very remote that few scientific expeditions had ever been there, and it was certain that all specimens and data which we obtained would be of considerable interest and scientific value. It was therefore expected that the American Museum authorities would look with favor upon someone pioneering this virgin region on their behalf.

Morden was an experienced hunter, having previously won his spurs in Nepal, Tibet, Kashmir, and India as well as in Indochina, Africa, and North America. He knew big game and he knew people. Accordingly he was ideally equipped for the task of organizing and leading such an expedition, and I was qualified to assist him in the collecting and preservation of the valuable specimens we would obtain, especially a complete group of *Ovis poli*, which was number one on our list. After we agreed to a basic plan and I said I would accompany him if the Museum authorities consented, he approached Henry Fairfield Osborn, president of the Museum, and Roy Chapman Andrews, who had already carried on several American Museum Asiatic expeditions much farther to the east of this area. As we expected, they heartily endorsed the idea, especially as Morden was to finance the entire project. Months were spent in planning, buying equipment, and getting passports and visas to take us into and through these "touchy" countries.

The time finally came to leave New York and head for Srinagar, in the beautiful vale of Kashmir. Here we spent the month of March, 1926, organizing our equipment and coolies for trekking over the Himalayas. For thirty days we foot-plugged it over many high snow fields and passes, a full month before they were considered safe for travel because of the treacherous spring avalanches.

With the last and highest pass (15,000 feet) behind us we dropped down into Sinkiang, not far from the Pamir border where we were to hunt.

We planned this trip into Central Asia for a period of five months, took two months' provisions, and stayed nine months. In all we covered about 9,000 miles, 3,000 of them entirely by native conveyances, riding horses, yaks, or camels, and then by native carts and sleighs for the latter part of the journey.

We were perhaps the first Americans and possibly the first white men ever to go right across Central Asia from Bombay to Peking. Now over the Himalayas and in Sinkiang, the land of the Kirghiz and Kazakh nomads, we moved westward up a long, narrow valley and camped below another high pass. Here we were met by a group of Kirghiz headmen, dispatched by the Chinese officials to welcome us and supply us with transportation and guides. Peyik Pass, as it was known, lay on the borderline of Russian Turkestan at 16,400 feet, and just beyond were the Pamirs, where we would find the Poli.

In no time, however, a mumble of misgivings arose among our men concerning the advisability of our going into this Russian country. They told us that we would run into "very bad people who would probably rob, if not kill, us." Whether they meant the Russians or the natives we were not sure because of the difficulty of conversing through a chain of interpreters. We had heard that no Europeans (except the Russians) had been in this country in sixteen years and that no Americans had ever been there. For three days we questioned our men and pondered the risk. We were told that there was a small Russian outpost a full day's march from the other side of the Pass. Bill and I then decided to send our Kashmiri guide and two local Kirghiz to the post with our passports, which carried Russian visas. This was a hazardous thing to do but it seemed worth the gamble. If our men did not come back, we would have lost both our men and our passports but we would still be alive. If they did return—then what? For this answer we just had to wait.

We dispatched our three men with good wishes and waited. At

the end of the second day we spotted four riders mounted on yaks coming over the Pass. But why four, we wondered. Could the travelers be our men or were they just local natives? Time proved them to be our own men accompanied by a native whom the Russians at the post had sent along, apparently to look us over.

Our men had presented our passports and told all about us as best they could, but still there was no definite answer about just what we could or should do.

After another full day of palaver the native from the post said that he would take us back with him. Although still uncertain what our fate might be, we decided to go. Cold, clear weather favored us for the stiff, steep climb up to the Pass, but as we began to descend the heavily snow-blanketed western slope we were often halted by blinding mountain blizzards. When it cleared we could see our Pamirs—a vast area lying under a blanket of white that resembled a newly frosted cake, with not a single dark rock or ledge breaking its immaculate surface. It was a forbidding land.

Going was heavy until we leveled off on the high, flat valleys and headed for the post. We saw a half-dozen horsemen riding straight toward us. As they came along at high speed we dismounted and waited, but not without some reservations. When they came close we could see that they were soldiers from the post. They were armed with sabers, rifles, and pistols. One carried a small machine gun.

What this all meant we did not know, for the soldiers were very stern and businesslike. Forming a line confronting us, one of them drew a large scroll of paper from his padded jacket and read it aloud. It was so long and monotonous that I remarked to Bill that it sounded like our death warrant. When the soldier had finished we asked our English-speaking guide what the message was all about and he replied, "It is a greeting of welcome, Sirs." And we gave a long sigh of relief.

They took us to their post, a very small group of adobe barracks surrounded by an adobe wall standing alone in the center of nowhere. Here we were seated at a long table with three or four of the higher officials and questioned at length concerning our purpose in coming to this remote place. They seemed to think that all we said about hunting the Poli was mere camouflage and that we were really looking for gold or planning to build a railroad. When they finally appeared convinced that we were really after their wild sheep, their spokesman said: "How many do you want?" Fearing to ask for too many we hesitatingly replied: "Ten." And he came back with: "What—only ten? You have come so far! Why don't you take a hundred?"

Thereafter we were permitted to go where we wished but we suspected that they always knew just where we were and what we were doing. Why our men had been so emphatic about these "very bad people" we could only guess. It could have been that perhaps from past mistreatment they just didn't like the Russians and were really afraid of them.

We had planned to get into this high country by May 1 in order to collect our specimens in their full winter coats. Our camps ranged around 12,000 feet and we hunted up to 16,500 feet and perhaps over that at times. The Pamirs, the summer pastures of the Kirghiz nomads, are not mountains but high, flat valleys surrounded by mountains which have long since eroded into rather smooth, immense hills where one can often ride to their very crest. And while these hills are often covered with much broken rock, there are few precipitous ledges. The Poli's grazing grounds are on these open hills, where they can see far and wide and take advantage of their undulating slopes should an enemy approach.

This high country being devoid of trees or bush, we burned "tezak," the dried cow-dung of the herders' cattle, for our fires. When this was absent or under snow we had to send our men miles to lower valleys to get a very small, low, sagelike bush. Water was obtained by melting snow or from an occasional spring. The soil provided a fodder of sparse, short, sweet grass, but not infrequently we had to carry native hay for our pack animals.

Our guides rode horses or bullocks while Bill and I rode yaks. They made wonderfully strong hunting "ponies," and were delightfully easy to slip on and off. We had brought along Army McClellan saddles and bridles rather than suffer the sawhorse con-

James L. Clark on his hunting yak "Pegasus,"
in the Russian Pamirs, 1926.

traptions used by the natives; and the saddles were a godsend for
mountain-going on yaks, bullocks, or horses. At this time, May 1,
spring was just around the corner, with the thermometer dropping
every night to zero or lower, with often a hot midday sun between
ten and two o'clock. We were always on our way for the hunt before daylight. If the distance to our selected hunting ground was
far, we would start traveling an our or two before dawn, when in
the stilled air it was always bitterly cold.

But as the days passed the warm noonday sun began to clear the
valley floors of snow, and each day the snow line would be just a
little higher on the slopes. We hunted the large open valleys en-
circled by rounded hills. If we saw sheep, we would then plan
our stalk; if not, we would go to the tops of the hills and use our
glasses.

Stalking was made comparatively easy in this open country by
the undulations of the valleys and the hillsides.

There are three cardinal rules for sheep hunting: Don't let them see you. Don't let them scent you. Come down on them from above.

During that month's hunting we saw hundreds of old and fresh heads lying around deserted Kirghiz settlements, which evidently

Poli habitat in the Russian Pamirs. This shows the vast scale of Asia's topography and the wide, flat valleys which intersperse the towering mountains.

were their hunting camps, and there were many fine heads among them. One appeared to have been shot within a year and was still in good condition. The horns of one head measured 59½ and 58 inches, with a base circumference of 16 inches. But of all the horns which I measured I never found one that went over 61 inches. I wondered how it was possible for a *poli* horn to add another 14 inches to its length, as in the case of the world's record. It would seem possible in two ways: if a horn added another several inches at the tips; or if a horn for some reason described a far larger circle diameter than normal, and thus by increasing its periphery also extended considerably its over-all horn length.

I found the *poli* a light-boned sheep with rather long legs. Their special characteristics are their widely flaring horns carrying long slender tips, which when unbroken or broomed-off (and the latter is rare) give them their open curl and excessive horn length. As with the other Argalis, their horns are heavily corrugated yet surprisingly light in weight for so much horn material. When their horn tips are unbroken their horns spiral to curl considerably more than a complete circle.

At the end of our month's hunt we had seen some 1,600 *poli*—500 males and 1,100 females. Some might have been duplicates, but when this seemed a possibility we discounted them. It was only after the middle of May that we saw our first lambs. We collected a fine series of males, females, and young of different age groups as complete skins and skeletons, giving the American Museum perhaps the best series of *poli* specimens in existence.

Poli carry a body-color of pale grayish-brown or buff, which is sometimes sprinkled with whitish hairs. Along the sides of the body from elbow to flank runs a slightly darker, broad stripe, dividing the body-color from the lighter under parts. The face, throat, chest, lower legs, under parts, and rump-patches are a light cream-white. In winter the longer hair on the neck and front of the throat forms a suggestion of a white bib—not noticeable in the summer coat. The back of the neck bears a thick cape of long, woollike hair starting at the base of the horns and ears and tapering backward to the shoulders, where it fuses with a narrow strip of long hair running along the medial line of the back to the tip of the tail. This same cape partly shows in the side view of the Arkal Urial photograph above. I am inclined to believe this a feature of all wild-sheep pelage, seen at its best when in their full winter coat. The horns are dull yellowish-white in color, much the tone of old ivory.

Bill Morden made some interesting observations of *poli* coloring under varying light conditions: ". . . winter pelage, [in] heavy coats making them appear larger and heavier than they were. In early morning light and at a distance, *poli* appear a creamy white with brownish saddles. Closer examination confirms the first impression except that between the white and brown there is an intermediate grayish tinge, which blends the two and runs up the back of the neck. The gray fades out just back of the horns, where the hair is almost white. In bright noonday light, when the mirage makes all objects at a distance indistinct, countershading will sometimes cause a band of *Ovis poli* to become almost invisible against slides of broken rock, not over two hundred yards away."

This description was made in the latter part of the month of May when the sheep were still carrying their heavy winter coat, and although the hair was long, it was often badly rubbed and considerably faded. I am inclined to believe that Bill's mention of the "saddles" may be explained by the fact that when animals are old the white of the neck and rump spreads beyond its normal limits over the shoulders and rump. This would then lessen the area of the body-brown making it appear like a large-sized saddle, but it has no connection with the saddle-patch of the Urial—for in this case the saddles are lighter, not darker, than the body-color. Although adult *poli* horns invariably form more than a complete circle, the world's record being 75 inches for the over-all horn length, their base seldom exceeds 16 inches. There are only three records of their going over that circumference, two being 16½ and one 17 inches.

Poli horns are relatively thin and triangular and therefore comparatively light in weight. The horns and skull of the specimen taken by the author weighed, when dried, but 25 pounds. An American Bighorn will go to around 40 pounds, while the *Ovis ammon ammon* horns and skull shown below weighed in at 49 pounds.

Poli and their near-by relatives are definitely of the "low-brow" type, as will be noted in several of the side-view pictures in this book, particularly those of the Littledale head.

The two photographs below show a ten-year-old ram taken in the month of May. He is still carrying his winter coat but is very thin, having used up all of his winter fat and as yet having very little if any new grass to nourish him. This specimen was dropped

James L. Clark and his 56½″ Poli ram,
taken in the Russian Pamirs, 1926.

in his tracks while he was seeking tiny tufts of old grass on this rock-strewn surface.

The *poli*'s habitat in the Russian Pamirs is far more arid and barren than are the sheep grounds of the Tien Shan and other mountain ranges to the northeast. Under fair weather and favorable ground conditions we had a rare opportunity to obtain many carefully taken measurements. This, the author's ram, went: S.H. 44″; H.L. 56½″; H.B.C. 16″; H.T. 42½″. The horn-circle diameter was 16½″, and the over-all skull length, 12¾″. The scales registered a total weight of 234 pounds. When weighed the specimen was completely devoid of fat, and there was little in his stomach. He could well have added another 60 or 70 pounds of fat during the fall to go to 300 pounds, or more.

Seven *poli* skulls measured an average of 13⅜ inches, the largest going to 14 inches. Our American Bighorn run in skull length to around 12½ inches. My recording of skull lengths in the appendices is based on the belief that a comparison of this particular measurement in sheep provides a better reading of their relative sizes than do their shoulder heights. Not only are shoulder heights seldom taken, but they can vary so much even when taken by experienced hands that they are quite unreliable.

In the following article, "The Legend of Chapchingal," my good friend Elgin T. Gates, of California, tells of his hunt, with a friend, for the *Ovis poli* in November, 1959. His story, which he has so generously permitted me to use in this book, eloquently speaks for itself; thus I shall say no more but let my readers enjoy it:

"The Legend of Chapchingal"

Have you seen the heart of Asia; do you know that lofty peak
  Where the Karakoram meets the Hindu Kush?
Have you seen the snowy fastness; it is there I go to seek
  For the mighty Ovis poli *known as Roosh.*
Do you know the weary travel; have you felt the howling winds
  When they clutch with icy fingers and harass?
Do you know the endless marching and the hope at every bend
  Pushing onward 'til you reach that lonely pass?
Do you know the hand that leads me; toiling thru this frozen waste
  Where the trail is lost in deep eternal snow?
Do you know what drives me onward; I must make that final chase
  For the hunter's horn has called and I must go.
Tho I've searched my soul for reason, I have sworn a sacred vow;
  Then I looked into the heavens for a sign.
Now the ends of earth are nothing; and although I know not how
  Still the horns of Ovis poli *will be mine.*

Deep in the heart of Asia where the Himalaya, Karakoram and
Hindu Kush ranges converge there stands the stupendous mountain of Godwin Austen, sometimes called K2. Its eternally snow-
capped summit rises 28,280 feet into the heavens. Few men have
looked at this awesome mountain. Fewer still have lived to tell
about it.

Ninety miles to the north as the crow flies there is a high pass
called Chapchingal. The men who have been there could be
counted on the fingers of one hand.

From the top of this 20,600 foot pass one can look down into
China. To the south lies Hunza and Pakistan. To the west is
Afghanistan and Russia. The valley going down into China is
called Taghdumbash. This is the home of the mighty *Ovis poli*.

There is a legend that when the hordes of Genghis Khan swept
over Asia all living things in their path fled or were annihilated.
The *Ovis poli* retreated to the valley of Taghdumbash. Once each
year when the snow lies deep in the valley below a great ram climbs
to the top of Chapchingal pass. If the sky is clear the summit of

Godwin Austen can be seen 90 miles to the south. Then—so the legend goes—the great ram will return to the flock and lead them back to feed on the dry grass uncovered by the howling winds that blow the snow into China.

When big game hunters gather to discuss the far corners of the world the conversation will inevitably turn to the *Ovis poli*, indisputably the most magnificent big game trophy on the face of the earth.

Shrouded in mystery and legend; spoken of in awe and reverence; their very existence is sometimes doubted. Yet they do exist in an incredibly barren land at an average altitude of 16,000 feet. Their habitat is called Bam-i-dunya, the mysterious "roof of the world," a land which has seen fewer changes, both in its aspect and inhabitants, than any other since the birth of the human race.

Thirteen hundred years ago this country was first described by Chinese pilgrims who said that "it was midway between heaven and earth; the snowdrifts never cease winter or summer; the whole tract is but a dreary waste without a trace of human kind."

Marco Polo, the greatest traveler of all time, crossed this country seven hundred years ago. He described it thus: The plain is called Pamir, and you ride across it for twelve days together—finding nothing but a desert without habitations or any green thing, so that travelers are obliged to carry with them whatever they have need of: North-east you travel forty days over mountains and wilderness, and you find no green thing. The people are savage idolators, clothing themselves in the skins of beasts: They are in truth an evil race. There are numbers of wild beasts—among others wild sheep of great size whose horns are a good six palms in length. From these horns shepherds make great bowls to eat from, and they use the horns also to make folds for their cattle at night.

Marco Polo was laughed at, but his tale was vindicated five hundred and eighty one years later when an English explorer named Captain Wood found a pair of *Ovis poli* horns and took them to England. It was named the *Ovis poli* or Marco Polo sheep in honor of the great traveler.

When the home of the *Ovis poli* became known to civilization after Captain Wood's exploit, men began to dream of going there.

In the beginning, the first sportsman to visit the Pamirs and shoot *Ovis poli* was St. George Littledale, one of the great British hunters of his time, and for that matter, any other time. In 1888, after great hardship, he came to the heart of the Russian Pamirs from the north via Samarkhand. When the spoils of his chase—the great curling Poli horns that measured up to 60½ inches were displayed in England, they created a sensation. The Poli country became the Mecca for big game hunters and so it remains to this day.

To this day too, it remains one of the most inaccessible places in the world, both physically and politically.

Littledale returned in 1889, and that same year another intrepid Britisher, Major Cumberland, crossed over the Karakoram range from Kashmir into the Chinese or Taghdumbash Pamir and collected *Ovis poli*. Later in the year he pushed on into the Russian Pamirs and by an incredible coincidence met Littledale on the Poli grounds.

A few more hardy hunters followed their tracks but time was already running out. Three years later in 1892 the entire region became permanent Russian territory and the Iron Curtain closed. This country became forbidden ground to all sportsmen. Only a few scientific and political expeditions into this country have ever been permitted.

This left only the Taghdumbash Pamir open. During the next thirty years only a few venturesome sportsmen had opportunity to hunt Poli. They were mostly British officers on leave or military business which took them over Kilik or Mintaka passes from Hunza into the Sinkiang province of China.

Here, near Kilik pass three great empires met—Russia to the west, China to the north and east, and India to the south.

In those early days Poli were plentiful in the Taghdumbash Pamir which lay just to the east of Russian Territory, but time was running out here too. Harassed by hunters and the native Kirghiz—who were learning the use of firearms; decimated by rinderpest;

pursued and killed by wolves and snow leopards; the Poli retreated westward in the fastness of the Russian Pamirs and finally disappeared from the Taghdumbash completely.

The last known Poli here was a young ram killed by a British officer at Kilik pass in 1929. Thereafter they were presumed extinct in this country.

For many years it was believed that the remnants of the once great herds of *Ovis poli* existed only in the Russian Pamirs, isolated in an area where even the Russians would not go because of the wild tribesmen and their everlasting hatred for the Russians.

Poli horns have been picked up in the Wakhan strip, a valley to the south that separates Russia from Afghanistan, and reports indicate that they occasionally cross over from the Russian Pamirs during severe winters. Afghanistan has long forbidden travel in this area because of the bandit tribes over which they have no control to this day.

The first Americans to collect *Ovis poli* were Kermit and Theodore Roosevelt who organized an expedition in 1925 for the Chicago Museum. They succeeded in obtaining permission to visit the Russian Pamirs. They saw no *Ovis poli* until they entered Russia, and after some difficulty they succeeded in collecting a group for the museum.

Shortly thereafter in 1927, another American museum expedition headed by William Morden and James L. Clark of New York also managed to get permission to enter Russian territory. There they collected some fine specimens of *Ovis poli* including two very good rams with horns up to 57½ inches around the curl. They saw no *poli* until they entered Russia, and reported that the local Kirghiz had seen only an occasional *poli* on the Chinese side.

It has been thirty two years since Morden and Clark visited the Russian Pamirs. They were the last. They found *poli* plentiful then, but no one really knows what their status is now or how many are left. Perhaps the Russians could supply the answer, but they haven't. With one exception they have kept the Iron Curtain closed and bolted.

In the summer of 1957, Prince Abdorreza Pahlavi of Iran, a great sportsman, used his royal influence to arrange a poli hunt in Afghanistan's Wakhan strip where he shot a *poli* with 45 inch horns. Then he managed to pry open the Iron Curtain long enough to cross over into the edge of the Russian Pamirs where he shot another *poli* ram of 50 inches.

This then, is a brief history of what is known about the *Ovis poli* to date.

There are men who have spent a lifetime dreaming about the grandfather of all wild sheep, the magnificent *Ovis poli* of Central Asia; dreaming of the moment when they had conquered the stupendous mountain ranges that barred the way; struggled thru the snow and cold; toiled over the glacial moraines; suffered the hunger and hardships of the trail until they climbed the last high pass where the roof of the world lay open before them.

Herbert Klein is this kind of dreamer. I am another. Besides being dreamers we share a motto: "The man who wants to do something badly enough always finds a way—the other kind find an excuse."

After 15,000 miles of travel by every conceivable means we finally stood poised on the threshold of the *poli* country. The way had been long and arduous, with many tiring marches behind us. We had hunted for many of the rare and exotic big game trophies that Asia has to offer. Let it suffice to say here that some of these stalks were successful, others were not. They are stories in themselves—Let us now get down to the story of the great *poli* rams of Chapchingal.

Ninety six miles from Gilgit up the Hunza valley is the tiny village of Pasu. This was to be our jumping off point.

We had been delayed three weeks by a series of physical and political obstacles, and finally it was only thru the personal guarantee of the Mir of Hunza to Pakistan's President Ayub Khan that the way was cleared for us to proceed.

It was now October 28, and the winter snows were due any day. We had to make some decisions, and fast.

We had intended to be thru with the hunt and back in Gilgit by the end of October, but now at this late date it was a gamble with weather.

While waiting for final political approval, we had many discussions with the Mir of Hunza about the existence of *Ovis poli*.

Some things he told us were encouraging, others were not. Our original intention had been to follow the ancient caravan route which led thru Hunza valley to Kilik pass, and hunt for *poli* on the Hunza side of the pass, hoping to find a few strays down from the early snows in the Russian Pamirs.

The Mir quickly dashed our hopes in this direction by confirming that the last *poli* seen near Kilik pass was killed in 1929 and none had ever been seen there since.

After endless discussions with the Mir, two possibilities emerged: Twenty-two miles before reaching Kilik pass there is a remote, narrow valley called Khunjerab which branches off to the northeast. Following this valley it is fifty-five miles to the Chinese border.

The only people to visit this valley are the Mir's shepherds who take their domestic sheep and goats there in the summertime to graze.

At the end of the valley there are two steep passes that lead into China. They are called Khunjerab and Chapchingal.

Here at these passes during the month of April the Mir's shepherds saw a few *poli* coming over from the Chinese side to visit some small meadows just under the crest of the passes. Some years they did not see any. These *poli* were undoubtedly an isolated remnant of the Taghdumbash herds which had been presumed extinct in 1929.

The first snows in late September drove the shepherds out of the valley, and no one could say whether the *poli* remained in the passes or went back into China. Logic would indicate that the same snows would send the *poli* down into the lower valleys at the eastern extremities of the Taghdumbash Pamir.

The Khunjerab valley had never been visited in October due to the deep snows so this possibility offered only a faint ray of hope.

The other possibility was the Shimshal nulla, a valley that

branched off at Pasu to the east. It too led to the Chinese border at a point about 20 miles airline from Khunjerab and Chapchingal.

The Mir told us that perhaps once every five years a few *poli* wandered into the upper basin of Shimshal pass from the direction of Khunjerab. This was an even fainter ray of hope, yet these two valleys beckoned to us like bright beacons.

The Mir warned us that even he could not tell us what to expect. The journey would be very dangerous in November, and the least thing that could happen to us would be to get snowed in. The weight of the early snows would bring down many avalanches, and the valleys were devoid of villages or inhabitants. Food would be a problem, and in case of any trouble, rescue would be next to impossible. We would be completely on our own.

Perhaps we should have turned back then, but we did not. We talked and talked. The hunger in our souls for this great prize was greater than reason. Logic was overpowered by our desire. We cast the die. We would try, no matter what the odds. Klein and John Coapman, the man who had brought us this far, would go up the Shimsal, a distance of 25 or 30 miles to an altitude of perhaps 14,000 feet.

I would take the longer route—90 odd miles up the Khunjerab to possibly 18,000 feet. The reason was simple. I was 20 years younger.

We thought of the undertaking as a calculated risk, but in the greater sense it was a foolhardy gamble with the odds stacked heavily against us.

With the decision made, speed became mandatory. I quickly made up my kit: Sleeping bag, my 300 Weatherby Magnum, binoculars, two cameras, 20 cartridges, a few rolls of film, my arctic parka, and the clothes on my back.

The Mir gave me four of his personal men. One of them was the school master who spoke English. Another was Gulbast, an old man who was the Mir's personal Shikari.

At Sost, the last village before the entrance to the Khunjerab, we would recruit additional men.

I said my goodbyes to Herb and John, not knowing for sure

when or if I would see them again. They were preparing to start up the Shimshal the next morning.

That first day we marched 25 miles to Khaibar, walking across the glaciers and rock slides, riding the horses when we could. There was six inches of fresh snow on the ground at Khaibar. The temperature was 26° F., and dropping fast. The horses were finished, so the Master traded them for fresh animals.

The next evening we pulled into Sost exhausted, but spent half the night recruiting men. When we pulled out the next morning we were 28 strong. The village was stripped of manpower, and even the headman came with us. Fortunately the Mir had given the Master unlimited authority to commandeer any men or animals we needed.

Some of the men were started off with their loads before daylight and by 9 A.M. we had reached the mouth of the Khunjerab, about 9 miles from Sost. The horses were sent back as there was no longer a trail for them.

Two yaks had also been started from Sost, and we passed them on the way. The water was high in the Khunjerab but the plan was to try to swim the yaks back and forth across the river as even they could not climb the sides of the canyon where we had to go.

From this point we would be walking the last sixty-five miles to the border. I checked the altitude here. It was 10,400 feet. A heavy overcast was an omen of more snow. We hadn't seen the sun since leaving Pasu and I was not to see it again for 14 more days.

From that point on the way was pure torment. We would climb steep cliffs, sometimes hand over hand for a thousand feet, then be forced to descend to the river again. How the men did it with their loads I'll never know. I was in the best physical shape of my life, and had it not been for the previous weeks of walking and climbing, it would have been impossible for me to keep up with the pace they set.

These Hunza men were magnificent. They have been described by Eric Shipton as the finest climbers in the world, even better than the Sherpas. They proved it here, right in front of my eyes. I carried nothing, except occasionally one of my cameras or binoculars,

Courtesy of Elgin T. Gates
The rocky road to the Poli country.

but I had to force myself to the absolute limits of my endurance to
stay with them. We crossed several fresh avalanches, saw others,
and heard several that came down behind us.

They did not need to be pushed or cajoled as they realized all
too well the urgency of speed in this undertaking, and they never
faltered. Late that first afternoon from Sost we came down off a
high cliff to Shachkatr, which consisted of a stone shepherd's hut in
a small level place by the river. The men cast their loads down and
began making fires out of the dry willows to cook their chapatis.
It was 5 P.M. and the Master indicated we would camp here for the
evening. I asked him about the trail ahead and he said the next
huts were about 7 miles ahead at a place called Wad Khun. He
asked me if I wanted to continue and without hesitation I said yes.
He turned to the men and started talking to them. After about
five minutes of discussion the men picked up their loads and we
took off with the Master and I in the lead. The supper fires they
had built were still burning as we started up the steep wall of the
canyon. The Master explained that Shachkatr was the furthest
point anyone had ever gone from Sost in a single day.

69

At this moment we were welded into a single unit, sharing the same intensity of purpose. The *esprit de corps* was born that was to be our ultimate salvation. The sore backs and muscles were forgotten. They would have something to tell about; to brag about when they got home. The gauntlet had been cast down. In their pride they picked up the challenge. Thereafter we moved as fast as human muscle and bone could go.

We rolled into Wad Khun in just under three hours. In a total of 14 hours we had crossed 23 miles of the most difficult terrain I have ever seen.

About 10:30 P.M. the two men and their yaks came stumbling in. They had nearly drowned crossing the high water of the Khunjerab and were totally exhausted.

When we awoke the next morning there was a driving snow, but we left as soon as it was light enough to see. The yak men were caught up in our driving spirit and we soon crossed the Wad Khun pass which is 14,000 feet and descended into the valley beyond. We stopped for a brief rest at Dih which is normally a 2½ day march. Here we crossed the Khunjerab river for the first time. I rode across on one of the yaks, and the men pulled off their skin boots and waded thru the cold glacial water. We pushed on that day to a point about 2 miles from Bara Khun, which is normally a four day march from the mouth of the Khunjerab. The valley grew narrower and the river had dwindled to the size of a small stream, and had become fordable. We crossed it a dozen times or more, and sometimes the men went barefooted to the next crossing rather than put their boots on to walk a few hundred yards, then take them off again. It was incredible how they withstood the icy water. It snowed continually during the day, building up. According to my maps we had traveled 21 miles in 16 hours.

The next morning we reached Bara Khun. Here it was 12,000 feet. There was more fresh snow, and it continued snowing throughout the day.

However, victory was in sight. The snow had not yet built up enough seriously to impede our progress, but there was enough to make the footing treacherous on the rocks. If nothing happened, we would be at Kuksell on the evening of the third day, something well over 65 miles including the ups and downs. Kuksell, the Master told me, was the last shepherd's camp and was approximately 6 miles from the Chinese border.

My map showed the terrain fairly well to Khunjerab pass, but Chapchingal pass wasn't even shown, and the areas beyond Khunjerab were blank and marked with the cryptic note "unexplored."

Also, according to the map, Kuksell stood at 15,800 feet. This was at the bottom of the valley, and around us the peaks rose up to the 23,000 foot level. We occasionally saw them thru a break in the clouds. A few miles after leaving Bara Khun, Gulbast, the old Shikari, spotted a herd of Ibex ahead just leaving the stream to climb the slopes. There was a bend in the canyon which made a perfect stalk possible. I quickly pulled my 300 Magnum out of its case and Gulbast and I made the stalk. We eased up to a little ridge and looked over. Four of the biggest billies in the herd were slowly walking up the bank of the stream. It was an easy shot at about 200 yards. I picked out the largest and dropped him in his tracks. The others fled up the slope then foolishly stopped after a hundred yards to look back. I picked out what I thought was the next biggest and squeezed off another shot that broke him down. He rolled almost down to the creek still threshing so we hurried up and I put the clincher in.

These Ibex were a different breed than the Ibex we had shot at Gilgit and Pasu. The horns were extremely massive like those from the Tien Shan range far to the north. The first one taped a shade over 47 inches around the curve and the second 46½. They were two fine trophies.

About 4:00 P.M. that afternoon, as we were nearing Kuksell, I saw something sticking out of the snow that raised my blood pressure to the sky. It was an old weatherbeaten skull and horns of an *Ovis poli*.

Up to this moment I still couldn't bring myself to believe there was any *Ovis poli* closer than the Russian Pamirs, yet here was physical proof. I pulled it out of the snow while the men gathered around. They pointed at it and said "Roosh!" and then they pointed on ahead up the valley and said "Roosh!" again.

It is hard to describe my emotions, but hope, which had been a faint tenuous thing in my heart, suddenly took wings and soared to the heavens. I fondled those old horns like a miner would fondle a gold nugget as big as a washtub. They weren't exceptionally big as *Ovis poli* go, but to me they represented all the wealth in the world. For here were real *Ovis poli* horns, and the animal that carried them had been here or at least nearby. How long I handled and looked at those *poli* horns I'll never know, but the men were already far ahead before I came out of my reverie and hurried after them.

An hour later we were in Kuksell where the final branch of the valley led up to Khunjerab and Chapchingal, 6 miles away. There was a stone shepherd's hut here about 12 feet square. We quickly made camp. The sky had cleared somewhat and the temperature was dropping fast. At 5:30 P.M. my thermometer read 18° above zero, and when I checked it again at 8:30 it read 4° below.

There was no wood of any kind here and the men were gathering yak dung and Burtsa, a scrubby plant that provided the only fuel at this altitude. It had a short heavy tap root and burned quite well. We leveled a small place under an overhanging boulder for my sleeping bag and the men quickly built a low wall out of loose rocks for shelter. All 25 of the men somehow got into the hut and slept there, keeping three small fires burning inside.

I crawled into my sleeping bag clothes and all, then pulled my arctic parka over my head. I was warm enough but couldn't sleep a wink all night.

I kept thinking about the *poli* horns I had found and asked myself endless questions I could not answer. Would there be *poli* in the pass or had they all gone back down into China? Would there be Chinese patrols there that were reported to make regular visits to the pass? Only the morrow would bring the answer, but at least, and at last we were here, on ground that *Ovis poli* had trod.

At 4:00 A.M. I got up and made ready. The temperature stood at 12° below zero and a biting wind had come up which I noted with some apprehension was blowing up the canyon towards Khunjerab. If there were any *poli* there the wind was taking our scent to them. I crawled into the hut, drank some hot tea and told the Master the plan I had decided on during the night. I would take him and the two shikaris; the man who had been carrying my camera bag, and one of the yaks.

We started up the valley at 4:30 A.M. It was barely light enough to see. About a mile from camp we ran into a herd of Ibex coming down to meet us. There was a tremendous billy carrying horns I estimated would go over 50 inches. He was within 75 yards, but I dared not shoot here.

We were climbing a steep incline now, and looking ahead I could see that the valley turned to the right. When we reached the bend, the valley opened out into rolling ridges and meadows that led up to the passes directly ahead.

We got behind some big boulders and I trained my binoculars toward the passes, about two miles away. There they were, Khunjerab to the right, the great glacier of Waaderin in the center, and higher up to the left, Chapchingal.

I then started scanning the slopes leading up to the passes. They were mostly covered with snow, but here and there were dark patches of ground where the snow had been scoured off by the wind.

I searched the slopes leading to Khunjerab for about five minutes then turned my binoculars towards Waaderin Glacier. Nothing. Then I looked toward Chapchingal and suddenly I froze. There they were! Nine *Ovis poli* rams with great flaring horns. My feelings were indescribable. My heart was in my throat, and my hands started trembling so badly I had to lower the binoculars. I am not ashamed to say that tears of emotion ran down my face and froze there. Here was a sight that few living men had been privileged to see. The magnificent *Ovis poli* in their natural habitat. It had been 30 years since the last one had been seen by a westerner; 32

73

years since the last *poli* was taken by an American Museum Expedition, and the first time in history that an American big game hunter had ever looked at these majestic animals.

When I had recovered sufficiently to raise my binoculars again I rested them on a boulder and feasted my eyes and my very soul on those great *poli* rams. There was no criterion to judge by, but I knew their horns would run well up into the fifty inch class.

Suddenly as I watched they threw up their heads and trotted over the pass into China.

My great elation turned just as quickly to despair. In my excitement I had forgotten the wind coming from behind us.

After a moment of indecision my mind started working again and I motioned the men to follow me. I led them about three hundred yards to the left against the slope behind some great boulders that had been spewed out from the Waaderin Glacier. There I tested the wind with some dry powdery snow. As near as I could tell the wind from this point was flowing up the slopes and would carry our scent just to the left of the summit of Chapchingal.

I started searching the slopes again and a few moments later I saw a great *poli* ram silhouetted against the sky on a ridge just under the crest of Chapchingal. Then followed a sight which transcended by far anything I have ever seen or hope to see in my lifetime.

His magnificent horns were clearly outlined, and were indisputably in the 60 inch class. He was slowly walking over the ridge toward us and just behind him came another ram, then another.

I stood there transfixed and counted them coming over the ridge single file, one behind the other.

Once again my emotions were indescribable. I kept counting—seemingly forever, until there were no more. Exactly sixty-five rams had come over that ridge; each one momentarily silhouetted against the sky. The largest rams were leading and yet the last one carried horns I estimated to be over fifty inches.

Think of this for a moment and perhaps the reader can understand the depth of my feeling at this awe-inspiring sight of 65 great *Ovis poli* rams in their prime winter coat.

I continued watching them until they reached an area where

the snow had been partly scoured away by the wind. There they massed together and started feeding. A few lay down and I saw others stamping through a thin crust of snow to get at the dry grass beneath.

Finally my hunting instincts came to the fore and I began to appraise the possibilities of making a stalk.

There was another ridge below them which was within shooting distance but to reach it we would have to cross at least a half mile of open snow fields in plain sight of the rams. Then too this would entail crossing the wind which was slowly increasing in velocity even as I pondered. Even from our present position a stray gust or eddy could easily carry our scent to them.

The possibilities of a stalk were quickly and irrevocably reduced to one. We would have to climb the slope to our left to see what chances were offered to get behind them in a down-wind position.

Just behind us there was a small canyon going up the slope which took us out of sight of the *poli*. I led the men into it and we started climbing. The way soon became very steep so I left two men and the yak there.

The wind here seemed to be blowing directly up the slopes and would not, I hoped, carry our scent to the *poli*. Here too, we left everything we were carrying except my rifle, cartridges, binoculars and a handful of dried apricots and a Chapati for each of us. I did keep my altimeter and thermometer in the inside pocket of my parka.

The four of us struggled slowly upward for more than three hours, occasionally working over to the crest of the canyon to mark the *poli*, which by now were all bedded down. We stopped to rest often and to get our breath back.

We would climb fifty yards, breathing four or five times with each step; rest for a few minutes, then resume the climb.

Fortunately, the little canyon led toward Chapchingal and finally I could see above us a snow-covered saddle with rocky pinnacles thrusting up a hundred feet or so on either side. This offered the only route so I studied it carefully and concluded that if we could reach this saddle and the terrain on the other side was passable, we would be in a position to work around behind the ridge where the *poli* were.

Breathing became more difficult and painful. My heart was beating with incredible speed, and the other three men showed increasing signs of altitude sickness.

Finally we struggled to the top of the saddle and stopped to rest. I pulled out my thermometer and altimeter which was a Swiss high altitude instrument calibrated to 21,000 feet. It now read 20,800 feet. With a shock I realized we were now standing on a place that was higher than any point on the North American continent. No wonder the men were getting sick.

A quick check over the saddle revealed an easy down hill slope behind Chapchingal. We were now in a position I estimated to be directly over the *poli*, but I could not see them because of the overhang.

As we prepared to descend I picked up the thermometer. It registered 14 degrees below zero. The wind had grown stronger and was now picking up the fine dry snow and blowing it out into space where it hung in a cloud.

We started down then, into China. Forty-five minutes later we had reached an outcrop that marked the ridge the *poli* had come over. Here we began to see *poli* tracks and droppings in the snow.

Staying behind the crest of this ridge we started downward again, paralleling the top of it. Luckily the wind had not changed and was coming over the ridge from the Hunza side from our right.

If the *poli* were still there we were now in a perfect position. Using the binoculars I could see the trail below they had made in the snow crossing over the ridge. The distance was about 400 yards.

Motioning the others to wait where they were, I crawled up to the top to see if I could spot them. I swept the slope with the binoculars, saw nothing, then inched forward a little more and slowly raised my head, and there they were, still bedded down. Crawling backward I joined the others and we started down again.

There was a large boulder about 50 feet below the ridge on our side at a point I estimated as being directly opposite the *poli*. We slowly crept up to the lee side of it and stopped. I wanted to check my rifle and rest here a few minutes to let my breathing settle down before making the final stalk. We sat down behind the boulder, facing toward China. As I checked the rifle and made ready, I began to wonder just what was going to happen when I went over the ridge. The *poli* were no more than fifty yards below the crest, and when I exposed myself to shoot they would obviously take off in a mad dash.

I didn't think I would have any trouble hitting something, but how to pick out a big one from the herd was the thing, particularly the tremendous ram that had led them.

Just then began a series of events that started out to be an incredible fiasco which later was to turn into an even more incredible stroke of luck.

Gulbast touched my shoulder and pointed. There were the *poli*, about 500 yards away just trotting over a ridge further into China. Somehow they must have seen me when I spotted them from above or, somehow sensed our presence in spite of the wind and the care of our stalk. They had gone down the ridge and crossed back below us out of sight.

Despair struck again and I cursed mentally. Then as I watched, the last seven or eight rams stopped just under the crest of the ridge and looked back.

I quickly decided to try a shot as this would be my only chance for a *poli*.

Moving around the boulder I rested the rifle on it, and took starvation aim at what appeared to be the largest ram. The rifle was sighted in for 300 yards, and ballistically the bullet would be $22\frac{1}{2}$ inches low at 500 yards. I allowed for this and gently squeezed the trigger.

The chosen ram took two or three leaps up the slope then collapsed and rolled back down to the bottom. At last I had a *poli*! I fired two more futile shots as the others ran over the ridge, then I began shouting with joy. The great quest was at an end! The men had caught my fever and we embraced each other then started running down the slope where the ram lay in the snow.

He was in prime winter coat and carried symmetrical horns that taped 52 inches on each side. Not too big as *poli* go, but I didn't care. He was a real *Ovis poli* and I never have to apologize for him.

After resting awhile I sent Gulbast down the valley to bring back the yak, the other men and my camera bag. I sent Aman Shah to the top of the ridge to keep a sharp lookout for any Chinese patrols who might have heard the shots, then the Master and I sat down beside the ram to wait.

About an hour later I heard something above and glanced up to see Aman Shah running down the ridge gesticulating wildly. My first reaction was that he had seen a Chinese patrol and I experienced a feeling of panic. When he reached us he babbled excitedly to the Master and pointed up the little nulla we were in.

The Master quickly translated that he had seen a herd of *poli* rams coming down-wind in our direction and that they would cross the nulla about 200 yards from where we stood.

I snatched up my rifle and started running. Just as we reached a rocky outcrop that extended out into the nulla I heard the rattle of rocks above. Looking up I saw a file of *poli* rams trotting down the slope.

I kneeled there and cocked the rifle. A few seconds later they plunged down the rocky bank and started across the nulla about fifty yards in front of me. It was point-blank range.

The great ram I had seen in the morning was leading the herd. My first shot was back a little but knocked him down. Then I swung on the second ram and got him, then the third. Out of the corner of my eye I saw the big one get up again so I swung back and took careful aim and dropped him for good with the fourth and last shot in the rifle.

Then I stood there in awe and watched the rest of the herd pour down the bank, cross the nulla and go over the ridge out of sight.

The big ram carried magnificent horns that measured 62⅝ inches on one side and 62½ on the other. The second ram measured a shade over 60 inches and third 56½.

My cup was full! The goddess of the chase had embraced me and handed me the greatest prize of all on a silver platter.

Courtesy of Elgin T. Gates

The big ram of Chapchingal Pass. Measurements: H.L. 62⅝″; H.B.C. 17½″; H.T. 47½″. Elgin T. Gates is in the middle behind the ram.

When Gulbast came up with the yak and the other men, we reconstructed what had happened by back-tracking the herd.

The first ram I had shot was part of another herd we hadn't seen, but while stalking the original herd we had come up-wind of where they had been bedded down in the nulla out of sight.

The original herd had never moved from where they lay until I fired the first shot, then they had run down into the valley away from us.

When Gulbast went for the men and yak, he had crossed up-wind of them and they had turned and come back in our direction. Had I not seen the second herd and fired, I would have undoubtedly stalked over the ridge into the midst of them, but the odds of picking out and shooting the big lead ram would have been next to zero.

There were further adventures with *poli* and a Snow Leopard, but this will have to be told later.

Let it suffice to say that the blizzard which had been brewing for several days finally struck with all its fury during the return march, and we barely got over Wad Kuhn pass, pushing through chest deep snow.

Arriving at Pasu I learned that Herb had been successful too, bagging two good rams up to 55 inches.

In closing, I can say only this: The mecca of any man is, in the greater sense, but the epitome of desire in his soul. There, in the heart of Asia, on a lofty wind-blown slope of the roof of the world, I came at last to my own mecca.

Hume's Argali

Ovis ammon humei

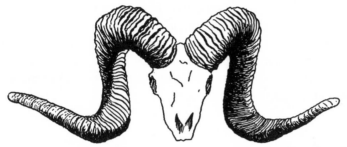

After Carruthers (1949)

Ovis ammon humei, sometimes called the Kashgarian Argali because of its close proximity to the ancient city of Kashgar, is perhaps the nearest relative of *Ovis ammon poli*.

Its range (see Map 3) is in the southwesternmost area of the Tien Shan, where these mountains begin to meld with those of the Pamirs, Hindu Kush, and Karakoram. This Argali is held by some to be extinct, but when I questioned Carruthers on this point he replied: "Why do you say *humei* may be extinct? Its territory is very secluded, very large, and not in danger of being developed, so far as I know."

Its horns are very much in the *poli* character but somewhat smaller and less flaring. Rowland Ward, in his *Records of Big Game*, lists the best horns as: H.L. 54½"; H.B.C. 15¾"; H.T. 35½" (taken by Carruthers). Because of its close proximity to the *poli*, it would seem safe to assume that it may be about the same in body-size and color.

The Tien Shan Mountains

The beautiful and spectacular Tien Shan, known since ancient times to the Chinese as the "Celestial Mountains," are roughly a twin chain running through the center Sinkiang and soaring to a height of twenty thousand feet and more. Heavily timbered with spruce and hardwoods, they are broadly bisected by a vast plateau

spreading between them. The plateau itself, ranging in altitude
from six to twelve thousand feet, breaks softly into many rolling
hills and valleys, generously watered by myriad glacial streams
offering rich pasturage for the big game and the natives' stock.

J·L·C·
THIAN·SHAN·MTS·
SEPT·1926

Resting ibexes. Ibexes were frequently encountered on the sheep
grounds of the Russian Pamirs and the Tien Shan Mountains. The
sketches show how the big males rest their heavy horns on rocks to
relieve the strain on their neck muscles. At right, a large male scratches
his back. Below, a young billy relaxes.

In this sheep paradise, particularly at the western end, wander
the *karelini* sheep, ibex, wapiti, roe deer, bear, wolves, snow
leopard, and wild boar, most of which may be had from one base
camp. Here, the *karelini* and *littledalei* sheep appear to overlap, to
confuse the hunter as to just what sheep he is getting.

In this rich grazing land Bill Morden and I found the Kazaks,
fine, sturdy nomads with blue eyes and light skin. Although they
herded many domestic sheep, cattle, and goats, their wealth was

in horses, of which they had great numbers. One group of horses we estimated to be of about one thousand head. Not only were these Kazaks good horsemen but they enjoyed the reputation of being good horse thieves as well. It was perhaps for this reason that when we first entered their domain, the governor of Sinkiang had dispatched a captain and a half-dozen Chinese soldiers to serve as a military escort while we hunted this Kazak country.

These soldiers were a motley lot with a variety of old guns, sabers, and sometimes pistols. Still, their very presence gave us considerable prestige and perhaps some protection. But our captain's face grew very red one morning when he found that horse thieves had come into camp during the night and got away with, among others, his very best saddle horse. They never did find the culprits or the horses.

Although the Kazaks seemed to be good people, we had difficulty in getting food from them. There seemed to be an ever-present hostility between the soldiers and the Kazaks, whom the soldiers treated with great contempt and arrogance. One day a group of Kazaks, taking us up to a good camping ground from where they said we could get sheep, hung around and even helped us pitch camp. When all was set and Bill and I had retired to our own tents, bedlam suddenly broke loose in the very center of our encampment. Rushing out to see what it was all about, we found the Kazaks mounted and attacking our unarmed soldiers with horsewhips and sabers.

We had no idea what caused this sudden explosion, but it was a furious battle. Two soldiers were completely knocked out and when I rolled one over and saw blood coming from his mouth, I said to Bill, "He's dead." In the midst of such a battle we feared for our own lives and were about ready to grab our guns, water bottles, and all our sweet chocolate and head for some high rocks to fight it out. As we hesitated, I saw them overpower the captain (all the rest of the soldiers, who had been brutally beaten, were now *hors de combat*). Two Kazaks grabbed him by each arm and held him helpless while one of the horsemen beat him unmercifully with his heavy whip. Another Kazak then drew the captain's sword from his belt, and I thought he was going to run him through. Bill and I believed that the Kazaks were subduing the soldiers first so that we could be more freely dealt with later. But now with the captain subdued there came a lull. We remained passive to let things quiet down.

When all seemed normal we called Hassan, our guide, to our tent and held court with three of the Kazak leaders to fathom the reason for this sudden outburst. It proved to be some unfinished business—vengeance—for an old brawl that had broken out a year before when these same soldiers had unfairly commandeered some of the Kazaks' sheep and food supplies, without paying for them. Apparently the soldiers then had the upper hand and the Kazaks just waited their turn, and this was the time for retribution.

The "dead" soldier came to in the night, and although all seemed quiet we never knew when trouble might break out again.

Sheep literature places the *humei*, *karelini*, *littledalei*, and sometimes the *poli* in this general region of the Tien Shan, creating a complexity nearly equal to that of the Urials in northeastern Iran. Here the range of the *karelini* is specifically given as the Alta-tau Mountains (location of type specimen) and the Lake Issik Kul region lying south of the Ili River and north of the Tien Shan, and also the adjoining Ak Sai Plateau or basin of the central Tien Shan. In *Unknown Mongolia*, Douglas Carruthers cites their distribution as follows:

"From N.E. end of Alta Tau Mountains, the karelini northern limit, westward along this range to the head of the Boro-Tala River and from there eastward along the whole length of the northern declivities of the range, up to and beyond, Hami, a small city of eastern Sinkiang."

It is said that *karelini* are also found throughout the central and southwest Tien Shan from the Eastern Yulduz (river) as far as the Ak Sai and Atbashi Plateau.

In color *karelini* and *littledalei* are noted as differing but little, variations resulting primarily from seasonal changes and age. My own *karelini* color impressions, derived from the pelage of the Chicago Museum ram, were recorded as: general color, grayish-tan

Sheep ground in the Yuldaz Valley of the Tien Shan Mountains. Sheep taken here may be either *karelini* or *littledalei*. When the author asked Carruthers how he told them apart, he replied: "I can't and I don't believe anyone else can!"

or buff thickly sprinkled with very small blotches of white hair resulting in an over-all speckled effect; face and muzzle whitish; neck at this time of year (summer) carrying no suggestion of a bib; ears very small, about 3¼ inches long; lower legs and under parts whitish, tail all white. Carruthers, in *Beyond the Caspian*, tells us that in winter these sheep grow a pure-white ruff (bib).

In the well-watered and more rugged Tien Shan our camps were tucked away high up in the side valleys where there was good water, wood for our fires, and grazing for our pack horses. Here, surrounded by big spruce and towering, snow-covered mountain peaks, we could well have been in a Wyoming hunting camp. Although sheep were plentiful among the broken hills of the plateau, we hunted for the big ones in the valleys above us. If the weather was cloudy, and it often was, we hunted the plateau below.

Showers, hailstorms, snow squalls, and sunshine punctuated every hour of the day, coming up over the near-by mountain tops to the south without notice or warning. All too often a good ram was lost in the fury of these sudden and unexpected storms. Many times I was marooned on a high rocky ledge, because it was too dangerous to move until the storm had passed.

Only scattered bands of younger rams and females now lingered in the lower basins, which had been vacated by the natives and their flocks in search of higher summer pastures. Above timber line were other steeper, more rugged areas of rich grassland where the nomads were now ranging their stock. This was by far the best sheep ground and the kind we had hoped to hunt, but we were deterred by the intrusion of the nomads. The big sheep that might have ranged here were certain to have retreated to more remote mountain recesses, not to return until the nomads had been driven out by snows. But by this time we too would have gotten out of these mountains and would have been on our way to other hunting grounds.

An Argali ram taken by the author in the Tien Shan Mountains.

The picture above shows a five-year-old Argali ram taken by the author in mid-September in the south-central section of the inner basin of the Tien Shan at an elevation of eleven thousand feet. More exactly, it was in the area or valley of the Yuldaz, a small tributary flowing northward into the Ili.

I have purposely refrained from naming this sheep, for frankly I am unable to say whether it is a *karelini* or a *littledalei*, but on geographical grounds it seems quite certain to be one or the other. At first I was certain that I had a *karelini*. But my companion, Bill Morden, decided later that it was a *littledalei*. I include it here because it is at least a good picture of an Argali.

This particular sheep was one of a band of rams that had long been studied through my glasses while I waited for a good chance to move to closer range. I made many pencil and mental notes, particularly concerning color, and here quote from my diary:

"They are a pretty sheep; a rather gray brown with a dark stripe running from the elbow, where it is perhaps 4″ wide, in quite a quick taper to the flank. The legs appear all white and the neck is whitish clear back to the shoulders, giving the 'white-neck' appearance of an old bull caribou. It looks also as if the hair on the front of the neck was long, making sort of a bib. The face is a darkish gray with a muzzle conspicuously white. In all, their markings were rather vivid for a sheep."

At this time (early fall) their new winter coats already had a good start, with rich coloring, which accounts for their markings' being "rather vivid for a sheep" and also explains why "the hair on the front of the neck was long, making sort of a bib."

Apparently most of the Argalis carry their white bibs only during the winter, shedding them with their long-haired coats in the spring. The exception to this rule is the Tibetan Argali, which carries a white bib throughout winter and summer, as reported by many hunters who have taken them during the summer months. But quite naturally they would then be much reduced in size, while probably being of a yellowish white color.

There are many references to the coat's being "very short" and this must be true, for the summers in these areas are brief but very hot, as most field notes have observed.

Although this ram was a comparatively young animal (five

years old), he was very large (44 inches at the shoulders). Except for horns and size he appeared no different in body and color from a *poli*. This sheep had a horn length of 41 inches. Its locality was the rolling, grassy plateau, with some of the higher hills topped with rocky outcrops. This ten- to twelve-thousand-foot open plateau, the winter pasture of the Kirghiz and Kazak nomads, was below the timber line.

Karelin's Argali

Ovis ammon karelini

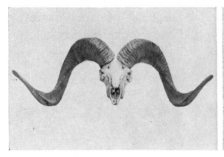

THIS SEVEN-YEAR-OLD *karelini* in the N.C.H.H., considered closely related to the *poli*, is therefore one of the Poli family. While the *karelini* horns look very much like those of *poli*, they are generally somewhat heavier in base measurement and have a somewhat tighter horn curl.

Rowland Ward, in *Records of Big Game*, gives the record head as: H.L. 53″; H.B.C. 16½″; H.T. 33¼″.

The Chicago *karelini* head below appears far more massive than the *karelini* pictured above and shows a much heavier horn than any *poli* horn that Morden and I observed in the Pamirs.

Courtesy of the Chicago Natural History Museum

Karelin's Argali (*Ovis ammon karelini*). This mounted specimen is obviously in his short summer coat, with a remnant of long winter hair in the shape of a Q on the side of the neck immediately forward of the shoulder. This "scar" is caused by the Argali's large, ranging horns which constantly hit the same spot as he turns his head. All of the big male *poli* collected by the Morden-Clark Expedition were similarly scarred. The "speckled" effect of the pelage, frequently mentioned in color descriptions of Argalis, is due to a sprinkling of white hairs throughout the darker areas.

In the summer of 1925, Theodore Roosevelt, Jr., and Kermit Roosevelt secured a fine *karelini* head in the Tien Shan with a horn length of over sixty-one inches, a probable record. I will let Kermit tell you the story of this hunt, which I here quote from their book, *East of the Sun and West of the Moon*:

"Kermit Roosevelt Hunts the Karelini and Gets a Record"

On August 15 Ted and I set out in opposite directions from camp. Khalil and Tula Bai were with me, while Ted had Rahima and a shenzi named Nurpay, the possessor of a remarkable pair of eyes. Our Kazaks wore hide breeches, and many a ride in the rain had bagged them abnormally at the knees. They reminded us of Father's story of how on the station platform at Medora, North Dakota, a slightly intoxicated stranger walked round and round his ranch foreman eyeing his leather trousers, and finally broke out with: "Well, if you're going to jump, jump, damn you!"

We rode cautiously along, dismounting below the crest of each hill and crawling to the top, field-glasses in hand to spy out the country. The first wild animal to be sighted was a marmot sitting at the mouth of its burrow. These dark-skinned little fellows are much sought after by the Kalmuks, and we were told that at Kulja a good hide would bring three dollars. At ayalik, when after ibex, I saw three of them tumbling about in the grass. One adult female I measured was thirty inches over all.

The next game we caught sight of from a subsequent rise was a roe-deer. Tula Bai informed me that it was a tika-illik—an ibex-roe—that its mother had been an ibex and its father a roe; but as a careful examination failed to show us any signs of this unusual mésalliance in the offspring, we decided to leave it alone for fear of disturbing any Karelini that might be within hearing.

Not long after this Khalil made out a small ram climbing up a steep hill. When it had topped the crest, we hurried after it. There were a great many crows on the hillside wheeling and clustering most agitatedly. It was evident that there were some disturbers of the peace in the offing. As we got nearer, we found that a brown hawk, lighter in body than any crow, was endeavoring to make a kill. He invariably attacked the crows upon the ground; six times I saw him swoop unsuccessfully. Half a dozen crows followed in his wake, attempting to mob him, but he paid little attention to them, avoiding them with the greatest of ease whenever they seemed to be uncomfortably close. Our way led through the scene of the combat, so we dispersed the gathering.

At the brow of the hill Khalil and I had our fieldglasses ready, and soon picked up three Karelini rams, feeding on a patch of grass a mile or more away. Our first stalk was a failure. Verily in this country "the wind bloweth where it listeth," and a sudden eddy made our quarry suspicious. They could have got only a very faint whiff, for they trotted off slowly while we watched them from behind a rocky ridge. We saw that in addition to the three marked down there had been as many more hidden. One was Khalil's small ram, and the others were clearly big fellows; Khalil and Tula Bai estimated them as all having horns more than fifty inches in length. Although they were between five and six hundred yards from us, Khalil was eager for me to open fire, insisting that I would get no second chance. His judgment of the proper time to shoot was very often faulty. Trotting across a narrow valley, they climbed a long, easy, sloping ridge. As they crossed a stretch of snow their horns stood clearly outlined, and we realized that those of the last one were larger than the others; but it was when he clambered upon a rock ridge crest and framed himself against the blue sky that we saw him in his full glory and appreciated his true size. Khalil turned to me: "If master get him, I give God twenty rupees at Bandibur!"

Tula Bai, although ready to go anywhere on horseback, was not of much use on foot; in addition, he was inclined to be crotchety and opinionated, so I sent him back to the ponies. When the sheep passed out of sight, Khalil and I made all speed toward where we had last seen them. We found that they had stopped seven or eight hundred yards farther on; some were lying down, others were feeding. The only way to get within range involved a long detour, and included some stiff climbing. An hour's work, the most disagreeable part of which was the crossing of two wide and steeply inclined snow-fields where we started a couple of small avalanches and felt in a very precarious and uncomfortable position, brought us to a ridge running down near where the sheep lay. Now was the time to make haste slowly, for a misstep and a loosened boulder would give us away. All went well and at a short 150 yards I fired.

We had picked out the old ram; he was lying down facing away from me, and I made precisely the same shot as I had with my ibex at Khanayalik. A bullet entering from behind and ranging forward is almost inevitably fatal. Although he ran, I knew he could not go far, so I turned my attention to his companions. I wanted four sheep. They ran off quartering and then swung around, uncertain whence the trouble came. Part of the time they were hidden in a ravine. I did some rapid shooting, fifteen shots, and when we hurried down to take stock we found that I had bagged five instead of four; one had fallen in the ravine without my knowing it. Only the small one got away. Ted said that whenever we shot at a number of animals it was, according to our shikaries, invariably a case of "The boys with their rakes killed twenty-five snakes, but the biggest one got away!" This time I had made any such theory untenable.

Upon measuring the heads we found that, although the four smaller heads were not as large as we hoped, ranging from forty-four to forty-six inches, the large one was bigger than we had dared to think possible. Around the curve these horns taped sixty-one inches. More than an inch larger than any head yet recorded. There was a great difference in coloration in these sheep. Our shikaries and the natives had told us that the darkest sheep were the largest, but in this case the big one had the lightest coat; three of the others were dark, and one light-colored.

It was four o'clock by the time we began the measuring and the skinning. We made out three Kazak herdsmen in a valley two or three miles way. Tula Bai gathered them in and we were glad of their help. Rain and sleet set in; skinning was bitterly cold work; but eventually I had two entire skins and three head-skins ready, and we packed them all over to the ponies across some very broken ground. On the ride back to camp Tula Bai took the lion's share of the load. On his pony he piled the two whole skins, leg-bones and all, roping a head on each side of the saddle, and perching himself on top. It was quarter to seven, very dark and cold and wet, but he set out undaunted in the lead. In places the ground was boggy and the ponies sank and struggled; elsewhere there were only rocks and holes, and dimly discerned precipices, along the very edges of which we skirted, but through it all Tula Bai's white pony, "like the crested plume of the brave Navarre," glimmered in our van. A white pony is a conspicuous hunting companion, and in the morning I had looked upon it with a very disapproving eye, but at night my feelings were altogether reversed. Khalil sang in Kashmiri and I in English and somehow or other the long, cold hours passed until half past nine, when we caught the glimmer of our camp-fire, after fifteen hours' hunting.

Littledale's Argali

Ovis ammon littledalei

SOMETIMES CALLED the "Kuldja"[1] Argali, the Littledale sheep, if not the largest, is one of the finest of Argalis. Its massive, spiraling horns, although running the larger Argali *Ovis ammon ammon* a close second, have all the qualities of a fine head. It ranges north of the Ili River from Kuldja to the Ala-tau Mountains, eastward along the northern declivities of the Tien Shan where it enters the central basin, and then eastward perhaps as far as Hami.[2] To the west it joins, if not overlaps, the range of *karelini*.

In color they are said to be not unlike *poli* and *karelini*, being a warm rufous-brown with grayish face and white muzzle and white around the eyes, while the back of the neck and shoulders are a somewhat darker shade of the body-color. The tail is a fawn color; there is no distinct dorsal line or flank band and no sign of the usual rump-patch, which makes it apparent that they are an evenly toned sheep.

Their basically parallel-beamed horns are massive and heavily corrugated, with a spiraled flare that often forms more than a complete circle. The measurements of the seven-year-old ram shown in the picture which appears earlier in this book are as follows: H.L. 57"; H.B.C. 15¾"; H.T. 40". The skull length of an adult Littledale ram will run about 13 inches.

[1] A small city and district on the Ili River in southeastern Russian Turkestan.
[2] A small oasis city in eastern Sinkiang.

Rowland Ward, in *Records of Big Game*, gives the world's record head as: H.L. 58½"; H.B.C. 16¾"; H.T. 45".

Their weight is given as 300 pounds, which would seem rather too low. Although I find no records of their shoulder height, their skull length will run a full half-inch longer than that of an American Bighorn, weighing in total 314 pounds. One could expect therefore that an adult Littledale sheep, with his more massive and heavier horns, could well tip the scales at 325 if not 350 pounds.

Ovis ammon littledalei appears to be the lowest of all the "low-brow" sheep.

Heins's Argali

Ovis ammon heinsi

After Carruthers (1949)

BEFORE WE LEAVE the Tien Shan there is one more, little-known subspecies of *ammon* for our consideration. This is Hein's Argali, a lighter-horned sheep, also of the Poli family. The validity of the kinship further adds to the sheep puzzle because it is said to range over much the same ground as *karelini* and *littledalei*. Some say it is now extinct, while others say it is a *karelini*. No one seems to know just what it is, and, like so many other sheep of uncertain status, it needs to be further studied and clarified.

Its range is given as the eastern part of the Alexandrovski Mountains of southeast Russian Turkestan and the area of Lake Issyk-Kul, north of Kashgar and southwest of Kuldja.

A comparison of the above line-drawing of one of these sheep heads with the photographs of its near-by relative, the *Ovis ammon nigrimontana*, pictured above, shows a remarkable similarity of horns, not only in the small base circumference but also in the wide, open flare. The *Ovis ammon heinsi* may well be the connecting link between the smaller Bukharan *ammon* to the west and the much larger *ammon* to the east.

Sair Mountains Argali

Ovis ammon sairensis

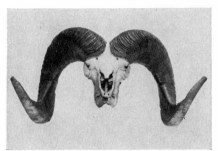

SOME TWO HUNDRED MILES north of Kuldja, in eastern Chinese Turkestan, in a most remote and little-known area, runs an east-west range of mountains known as the Sair, Saiar, or Jair. As reported by Littledale around the turn of the century, these mountains and their surrounding country form the home of this unfamiliar sheep, *Ovis ammon sairensis.*

This is another of the big, heavy-horned Argalis similar to the *karelini* and the *littledalei*; but because of its higher "brow" it appears to be more closely related to the eastern Argalis than to the Poli family in the west.

Although no record of their shoulder height is available, we can assume, from its 13½-inch skull, that this measurement would run from 44 to 46 inches.

The horn measurements of the ten-year-old specimen shown above are: H.L. 47½"; H.B.C. 15½"; H.T. 31"; Sk. L. 13½".

These horns show but a very slight divergence of the main beams, which is probably typical.

Douglas Carruthers (*Unknown Mongolia*) gives their range as "more northern, loosely attached outlying mountains north, east-west range of Ala-Tau and Barlik Mountains, branching off to the northeast from the west end of the Tien Shan. Separated from the Altai by the broad basin of the Black Irtish River."

Their color is described by Richard Lydekker (*The Sheep and*

Its Cousins) as follows: "In summer the whole of the upper-parts, with the exception of the white muzzle, as well as the upper portion of the legs are reddish fawn. There being *no* rump-patch, while most of the under-parts are darker. Females with a dark dorsal streak."

It is interesting to note that here we have a decided deviation in sheep color-pattern in the "no rump-patch" and "under-parts are darker," specific features which help to make their identification easier and perhaps more positive.

The Semipalatinsk Argali
Ovis ammon collium

THEIR RANGE is the Tarbagtai and the hills of the Kirghiz steppes of Russian Turkestan, bounded by the region of Semipalatinsk on the north, the Sair Mountains on the east, and Lake Balkhash to the south, with the province of Akmolinsk to the west.

Like *sairensis*, its remoteness makes it little known, and no photographs or measurements have been available. Being in lower, more arid country to the west, it is probable that because of its less favorable pasturage, it is a somewhat smaller sheep. It is believed that this sheep is now extinct.

Douglas Carruthers, in a letter to the author, writes: "*Sairensis* and *collium* are more difficult to place for they seem to be half way between the two [*littledalei* and *ammon*], but I should leave them as you have placed them [on Map 3].

"There is not the least doubt in my mind that *Sairensis*, named by Lydekker in 1898, from a few specimens from the Sair Mts. (an off-shoot of the Tarbagtai) is identical with *collium*, named by Severtzov in 1873 from *more* abundant material from the same area and its neighboring ranges. Therefore, I would put '*Sairensis*' [as] now considered to be *O. a. collium*."

The Siberian or Altai Argali

Ovis ammon ammon

IF A REALLY BIG RAM is the finest trophy a hunter can obtain, then this particular Argali is it, the *Ovis ammon ammon*, the King of Kings of all sheep—and well named, after the Egyptian deity Amen (Amon), depicted as a human body with a ram's head and horns.

Courtesy of Douglas Carruthers

The home of the Siberian Argalis. Here rich grasslands spread over the ten-thousand-foot Altai Mountains lying along the adjoining borders of Siberia, Sinkiang, and Mongolia.

Tribute is paid to this superb sheep by J. H. Miller in a chapter contributed by him to Carruthers' *Unknown Mongolia*:

"There are few species of big-game that appeal more to the heart of the hunter and lover of the wild regions of the earth, than an old ram in his upland solitudes. Apart from the magnificent horns he carries, his unrivalled wariness tests the resources of the hunter to the utmost. Luck plays a very small part in sheep-hunting; skill, patience, and perseverance are required to a high degree."

Some say that the Tibetan Argali (*Ovis ammon hodgsoni*) is a little larger in body than this *Ovis ammon ammon*, but the skull measurements which I have taken do not indicate this, the Siberian Argali skull being a full fifteen inches in length whereas the Tibetan *hodgsoni* is something less.

Although the few records that I can find give both of these sheep a shoulder height of forty-eight inches, there is little doubt that the *ammon* is the heavier of the two, for his horns alone far exceed those of the Tibetan Argali in mass, measurements, and weights. The shoulder height measurement of one *Ovis ammon ammon* is recorded at fifty-three inches, and this may be possible. Accurate shoulder heights are very difficult to obtain, even by experienced men, because in death the forelegs relax and extend far beyond normal. One can only guess how far to push them back up to their proper place before measuring, while indiscreet hunters, ever inclined to boast of bagging the biggest trophy, are apt intentionally to extend a front leg to its maximum before measuring.

These Central Asian sheep range over a vast area of country of which man can cover but a tiny bit at a time, and while a considerable amount of data has been secured, it is at best spotty and greatly in need of correlation. But this will take years and will be possible only if the wild sheep are fortunate enough to survive that long.

The range of this particular *ammon* is in the massive mountain uplift called the Great Altai, where southern Siberia, Sinkiang, and Mongolia come together.

To the north and west the *ammon* range as far as the area of Semipalatinsk, and to the southeast they stop on the fringe of the Gobi Desert. Previously *Ovis ammon ammon* were found in the mountains running eastward through southern Siberia just north of the Mongolian border, but today it is doubtful if they could be found very far from the northern Altai Mountains, where it is said that they have always been the most numerous and the largest.

As to color, Miller, again in Carruthers' *Unknown Mongolia*, says: "In autumn the coat coloration of an old *ammon* ram is very striking. The nose is white, forehead and cheeks grey-brown, neck and upper part of the body dark chocolate, freely sprinkled with white hairs, which slightly predominate on the shoulders and along the back; this gives them a very grizzled appearance. The belly and rump-patch are white, legs grey-mottled above and white below the knees. In full winter coat an *ammon* ram is of a dirty-white color on the body and neck, and pure white on the nose, legs, and rump.

"The *ammon* differs from nearly all other large Central-Asian Sheep in that he does not grow a long neck-ruff (bib). In summer the coat is exceedingly short, but in winter it lengthens all over the body and neck to about two inches."

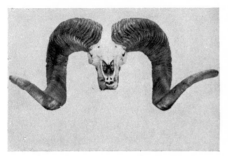

An *Ovis ammon ammon* head

Data on the above *Ovis ammon ammon* head, at present in the N.C.H.H. of the N.Y.Z.P.: age, ten years; locality, Altai Mountains, south-central Siberia and northwest Mongolia. Measurements: H.L. 59½″; H.B.C. 19½″; H.T. 41″. The skull length by calipers measured fifteen inches, a remarkable length, which gives some idea of this sheep's huge size. The outside diameter described by the horn's circle measured nineteen inches. For shoulder height and weight, we have no alternative but to accept the former as 48 inches and the latter at around 400 pounds, although it is my guess that the weight might run to 450 pounds when carrying winter's full blanket of fat.

This is a remarkably fine *ammon* head in every respect and appears very closely to equal, if not to surpass, the world's record taken by Littledale in 1900 (pictured above).

Comparative measurements:

Littledale head		N.C.H.H. head	
H.L.	61½″	H.L.	59½″
H.B.C.	20½″	H.B.C.	19½″
H.T.	37½″	H.T.	41″
Total	119½″	Total	120″

Whatever may be the pros and cons regarding their comparative excellence, they are both remarkable heads. The extraordinary skull length of 15 inches as compared with a 13¾ inch *poli*, which is known to stand 44 inches at the shoulder, shows how big these *ammon* really are. It would seem therefore that the figures of 48 inches at the shoulders and 400+ pounds for the *ammon's* weight must be well on the conservative side.

The weight of the N.C.H.H. skull and horns alone, thoroughly dried, was exactly 49 pounds, a very considerable weight to carry.

But if such immense horns are "carried with pride and dignity," as Demidoff states, they are also carried as a fatal impediment, especially when fighting belly-high snow. This is perhaps why some really big heads have been "pickups" on the mountain sides—as in the case of the world's record Poli.

The Morden-Clark Hunting Comes to an End

Once during an all-night forced march Morden and I passed a small amphitheater-like pocket near the trail. It was bare of snow and in its center, in the light of the moon, were strewn the skeletons and horns of five or six big sheep. Although most of the bones were parted, the vertebrae, separated from the skulls, were intact. Their locality and massive horns marked them unmistakably as *Ovis ammon ammon*. I pondered the reason for their concentrated death. Had they been killed by man or beast, they would have fallen singly and far apart and their bones carried off. It seemed evident that they had sought shelter from a severe storm—and tragically had been trapped by winter's deep snow and had died of starvation. I regretted our inability to take one or two of those fine heads, for they were in perfect condition.

This was when we were traveling by camel caravan over the Altai Mountains in the late fall of 1926, passing through this *ammon* country, which was under snow. Although we sighted sheep, there was no opportunity to go after them. Small wonder, for at the time we were prisoners!

* * *

On November 6, Morden and I were in the eastern end of the Gobi Desert, making a dash to get out of Central Asia before being snowed in for the winter.

We had left Urumchi by camel caravan about a month before, regardless of a warning from the governor of Sinkiang that their Mongolian border had been closed and that our trip would be a dangerous venture because of the extreme cold and the presence of bandit gangs along our route. In spite of the hazards we decided to go on our way and were now approaching the southeastern foothills of the Great Altai, heading for our objective, Urga, which lay some one thousand miles to the east.

Somewhere ahead ran the Sino-Mongolian border, but none of our men knew just where it was. A howling desert-blizzard had brought us to a halt, and we had to sit it out for the better part of two days huddled around the tiny fire in the cook's tent trying to keep warm. When the storm showed signs of clearing we made ready to move, but it was not until late afternoon that our thirty-five camels were packed and we started trekking over the frozen ground whitened with a hard layer of wind-packed snow.

As darkness began to fall it became bitterly cold. After painstaking preparation for an all-night trek to make up for lost time, we headed eastward "into the unknown," all trails having long since become obliterated. Such maps as we had were of little use, for they showed neither roads nor settlements. We hoped to run into occasional nomads to ask our way, but this was merely another of our many uncertainties. Only the stars by night and the sun by day would now give us our direction.

As the last faint rays of daylight began to fade I took my position at the end of the long line of camels in order to keep contact in the dark. Only the crunching of snow under their heavy loads and the plaintive tinkle of their wooden bells told me which way they were heading.

I had settled down for the cold, all-night grind, when out of the corner of my eye I picked up two indistinct objects moving swiftly along our right flank. In the dimming light I could not make them out but concluded that they must be wolves about to close in on us under cover of darkness.

Dashing up to the line to warn Bill to be on guard, I found him just pulling his horse to a halt. When I told him what I had seen, he replied, "They're not wolves, they're Mongols, and they're all around us." At that moment two wild-looking horsemen came dashing out of the dark directly in front of us and motioned us to halt. They were bareheaded and carried guns. While one came in close and lit a match to inspect us, the other skirted the camels to see what we were carrying. Then with much jabbering others moved in around us. A cold chill went up my spine. "Bandits," I murmured to Bill. We took out our flashlights and turned them on our faces so they could see that we were white men—but that did us no good whatever.

Knowing that we were outnumbered (there must have been eight or ten of them), we remained mum and helpless, fully believing them to be bandits who had waited for darkness to take us by surprise. Three or four of them surrounded Bill and me, our guide, our Bashi (caravan leader), and our personal servant Mohamed and rode us off into the black of night at breakneck speed. Why and where we were going we had no idea. After a few hundred yards they came to an abrupt halt and impatiently urged us off our mounts. In the faint light of the stars I could make out two yurts. We were hurried into the nearest, where half a dozen other Mongols squatted around a dim central fire. They were strangely indifferent, and the reflected light on their sinister faces struck us as anything but a good omen.

In a state of bewilderment Bill and I steeled our nerves and moved around to the "place of honor" opposite the doorway, squeezed into the circle of huddling Mongols, and lit our pipes. This was a face-saving gesture, an effort to hide our deep concern. But as in the lull before a storm, the air was loaded with uncertainty. Hindered by the limitations of our interpreters, we tried to explain our papers and prove that we were Americans, but this got us nowhere, even though our guide could speak some Mongolian and tell them something about us. We noticed that there was always one armed guard stationed at the doorway while others frequently came in, talked excitedly with the group, and then went out. Fully half an hour passed without incident, and then we heard the bells of our caravan trailing in. We ordered our men to go out and pitch camp. As they started toward the door, bedlam broke loose. Our men were knocked to the ground and tied up. Shouts and orders flew back and forth as more armed Mongols rushed in and out. Two coming in with ropes headed straight for Bill and me. Heavily outnumbered as we were, it was useless to fight back. We strove to remain calm rather than incite them to further violence. It was all in vain. We too were thrust to the ground, tied hand and foot, and rolled over and over while they searched our clothing and emptied our pockets. Then they really showed their contempt, kicking our men, spitting at us, crossing and tying our wrists together with rope, and finally pouring hot water on the ropes to shrink them even tighter. This was to induce pain, their age-old method of torture.

Helplessly bound and compelled to lie flat on the ground, we now had time to think. Our men were groaning. Blood gushed from the Bashi's mouth. The tightening ropes cut into our wrists. Pains shot up our arms and into our bodies like tongues of fire. If we lifted our heads or moved our bodies for some relief, we were promptly knocked back on the floor. We had no idea who our captors were or why they gave us this treatment. We asked our men what they were talking about and word came back: "They say they are going to kill us, Sahib." We could only hope that they would shoot us instead of torturing us to death.

Our captors continued an endless babble, while the slowly shrinking ropes pulled ever tighter about our wrists. Finally, after hours of excruciating suffering, we were motioned to our feet and out of the door. As there was little doubt that we were now headed for the firing line, we said good-by to each other. We moved out into darkness. Immediately we were surrounded by gun-bearing Mongols, and led into the open. Ahead was a tiny glow of light. It came from a tent. Into this we were pushed and again thrust to the ground. Our arms and wrists were still bound. Our men were forced to lie flat, while Bill and I were tied back-to-back in a sitting position to one of the tent poles. Our conclusion now was that they were safely lashing us up for the night and would dispatch us in the morning.

On the pole above our heads burned a primitive oil lamp, and we feared that it would drip and set our clothing afire. Watching over us was a surly-looking Mongol with an old rifle, which he pointed at us every time we moved to get some relief from the ever-shrinking and increasingly painful ropes. Sleep was out of the question. I tried to faint for some respite but could not. Sleep came only momentarily, and then one would awake with a start from some frightening dream. After what seemed an interminable night, a faint glimmer of light broke the sky. We wondered what lay in store for us.

At the crack of dawn an armed Mongol appeared at the tent door and beckoned to Mohamed. Shortly after he left we heard a single shot and I said to Bill, "There goes poor Mohamed, I wonder who will be next." And we waited and waited.

Then came the sound of crunching snow under heavy boots, and we broke out in a cold sweat. There in the doorway, like a ghost from the dead, stood Mohamed. When we found our tongues we asked him what had happened. He explained that they wanted him to open some of our boxes to see what they contained. The one shot we had heard was from Bill's revolver, which they had found and tried.

After some thirty hours of the rope torture they removed our bonds and let us go to our own tents. However, everything was taken from us except a few personal items and some food, which they allowed Mohamed to prepare for us. Thereafter although the "thaw" came very slowly, each day seemed to lessen the chance of our expected fate, but we were never quite sure. They would neither let us go on our way nor let us return to Urumchi. Our men told us that they heard that our captors had decided to deliver us into the hands of their big chief at a place called Kobdo, which was about 350 miles beyond the Altai. Our hopes were again dashed by despair, for it meant that we would probably not get out of Asia until the following spring, if at all.

On our first day's trek we were on the trail for eighteen hours, the last part of which was an all-night March, in zero weather, over three nine-thousand-foot passes of the Altai. It was on this trek that we saw the remains of the big *ammon*.

At Kobdo, still some 350 miles south of the Siberian border, we met a group of Russian traders and a Russian consul. To save face for themselves, these Russians took us over from the Mongol chief, under whom we had passed a full week of misery and suspense. The Russians promised that they would get us out of the Mongol country without further trouble and reminded us of our great good fortune in having been brought to Kobdo, where they could help us, instead of being summarily shot. At last, after another 350-mile troika-trek through Siberian forest in sub-zero December weather, we took the eastbound train at Novosibirsk for Peking.

At Urumchi, in anticipation of the risks we were taking, we had dispatched the last of our valuable Museum collection southward via India to America. And now, at Kobdo, we presented our camelmen with the entire caravan outfit to get back to Urumchi as best they could and gave the Russians our food, tents, and much of our equipment. We made our 350-mile trek to the Russian border with a minimum of baggage, but still under an armed guard to make sure we went there. From the time we left Kobdo until we took the train at Novosibirsk for Peking we were kept constantly under the suspicious Soviet eye as "house prisoners." And when we reported our experience to the American Embassy in Peking they advised us not to mention it to anyone until we were safely out of Asia.

It was some time before we managed to figure out why we had been so badly treated, but eventually the picture took form. Nine years had passed since the Bolshevist Revolution, and the Soviets were now beginning their program of expansion by subversion and infiltration. The countries to the east being the weaker, they were starting with Mongolia. China was already overrun by a "nationalist" army, which eventually brought about the expulsion of Chiang Kai-shek's forces from the mainland. The wild and independent Mongolians were proving a bit harder to crack; accordingly the Soviets, further to weaken them, first got them to secede from China and then began their process of infiltration from the west. We had already run into the "closed" Sino-Mongolian border and previously into several of the closed Sino-Russian banks of these countries, which had apparently been shut down by the Soviets to create economic chaos. Soviet agents and army officers were already in western Mongolia, brainwashing and training the natives as foot soldiers so that they could "defend" themselves against any "interference."

The Mongols whom we had encountered were some of these brainwashed locals who had been given arms to keep all "foreign imperialists" out of their country. Thus we were "spies" attempting to run the border under cover of darkness and deceit—and deserved to be punished, if not shot. Only because they had little authority did they pass us along to "higher-ups," which action perhaps saved our lives.

The Russian consul and a Russian commandant who were in Kobdo to train the Mongol foot soldiers were not a little aghast at the treatment which we had received from their Mongol "comrades," for it was then much too soon for such tactics to come to the attention of the Western world, since it would be unfavorable publicity for them. And so it was that we were perhaps the first Westerners to fall victims to the Soviet's first Iron Curtain.

Now we could better understand why our men had had such misgivings about going into Soviet-controlled territory.

"Douglas Carruthers Pursues the Ammon"

DOUGLAS CARRUTHERS in his book *Beyond the Caspian* gives a good story of an *Ovis ammon* hunt:

At very great range I spied through my glasses the great curling horns of a giant ram. He was alone and apparently asleep, but in an impregnable position on the top of a little isolated grassy knoll. I could see nothing except the horns, but presumably they were attached to a beast, for it was not a likely place in which to find a pair of derelict horns.

Courtesy of Douglas Carruthers

Carruthers' hunting camp in the Ammon country, where the steep, grassy hills drop off from the higher, rolling plateau.

He was solitary and therefore might be a monster, for the chances were that he was a very aged ram, who, being worsted in a fight to maintain supremacy, had retired to a lonely but more peaceful existence away from the herd. I had met such a one in the Altai, and he had oviously removed himself from his fellows—and the ladies—because he was so ugly. A battle-royal had damaged his nose so badly that a large scab had grown over the wound, and the resulting disfigurement entirely justified his action. Fighting had spoilt his beauty and so he lived alone.

The knoll was so isolated that there was no possible means of getting within shot of the beast, until one arrived there, literally on top of him. In due course I reached the flank and, with infinite care, crept up it. With even greater care I raised myself the last few feet, and finally the last few inches. As the grassy summit came slowly into view, I realized that there was nothing on it! But I saw to my astonishment that there was another knoll, *exactly* like this one, a little further on; and there lay my beast. It *was* a ram, a monster—and he was fast asleep.

The distance was still too great to risk a shot, so I had to repeat my assault on position No. 2. This time I took even greater care, for I now knew for a certainty that, if only the wind remained friendly, I was about to meet *Ovis Ammon* himself, face to face. In fact, I calculated that I should reach the crest of the knoll within a few yards of him—a unique experience.

I could hardly believe that my thumping heart would not wake him, as I crept up to where a solitary rock broke the skyline and gave some sort of cover. Otherwise the final approach was over the smooth rounded curve of a sugar-loaf-shaped hill. I could have no warning at all of just when the top of his horns would come into view.

I was quite close to the rock, when the silence was broken by a sudden stamp; a mighty pair of horns reared themselves above the rock—but I could see no more—the rock hid the rest of him from me, and all of me from him. The distance was about ten yards!

Our hearts stood still.

Trembling with anxiety, my eyes wet with sweat, I waited.

He took one step forward, exposed himself, and before he knew that Man was upon him, he died.

Not instantly though, for the range was so close my bullet

Courtesy of Douglas Carruthers

Ovis ammon ammon. "I had met such a one in the Altai . . . a battle-royal had damaged his nose."—Douglas Carruthers

drilled a tiny hole clean through him. He charged away and down the slope several hundred yards before he fell dead.

He was a fine specimen—a perfect one of his race.

The Littledale-Demidoff Hunt for Ammon

In the summer of 1900, St. George Littledale and Prince Demidoff, accompanied by their wives, hunted the *Ovis ammon* along the Siberian-Mongolian border in the extreme northeastern corner of Sinkiang. At the end of the first day's hunt they came in with no fewer than six big rams, one of which had a horn length of 52 inches and another of 49½ inches.

Their camps, which were tucked away in a small gully affording firewood and water, lay at an altitude ranging from seven to nine thousand feet. Above them rose the undulating, grassy plateaus where they would find the big *ammon*. At the time this was virgin country (they were probably the first white sportsmen to venture into this unfamiliar land), and bands of up to twenty or more sheep were seldom out of sight.

It was the usual hunting, up early and off by the break of day on their ponies or yaks with local Mongol guides following on foot. A short, steep climb up the stony gullies, and then the first careful peek over the top to survey every nook and cranny of the rolling hills. If sheep were sighted—and they usually were—each band would be carefully examined for big heads and either left undisturbed or further surveyed to determine the best strategy of approach. Ground swellings not easily detected were always danger spots, for from a seemingly flat plain a sheep might unexpectedly come into view, catching the hunter "hands down" right in the open. This and a sudden change of wind, always the uncertain factors of any stalk, inspired the party's slogan: "Keep low, move slowly, and be ready to 'freeze' in a split second."

In such open country it was not always easy to get above the sheep, so strategy had to change constantly as the approach progressed. Patience and urgency were ever in conflict, for both seemed of equal importance. When the hunters were within three hundred yards and could not safely shorten the distance, they had to wait until the sheep moved. But if they were lyingup for their midday rest, the hunters would have to circuit them for a mile or two for a better approach. At best it meant shooting at long range. Once in a while hunter and sheep would unexpectedly come face to face, to the intense surprise of both, as they mounted a little ridge or hilltop. Then it was snap-shooting at a very-fast-disappearing sheep. And it was amazing how quickly those sheep found some undulation to serve as a hide-out. However, there was hardly a day that the party came in empty-handed.

Then came the lucky hour when Littledale was to get his world's record *ammon*. He had been out the day before with Princess

Demidoff, and she had wounded a small ram in a band of some twenty or more. As the herd sped off, both she and Littledale had tried to bring down the ram but with no success.

Since Littledale was certain that the group held one or two very big heads, he planned to go back the next day in search of the same band and look them over. I'll let Demidoff tell you the rest of the story, taken from his book, *After Wild Sheep in the Altai and Mongolia*:

"Littledale Gets His World's Record Ammon"

LITTLEDALE AND MY WIFE had just returned. They gave me an account of how they had got within 200 yards of a herd of rams which were already on the move; she had fired five shots at the running animals, but none apparently were hit. Littledale added that he had noticed two or three magnificent heads amongst them, and was most anxious to go out next day in search of them.

Weather being fine, on the morning of July 29th, Littledale and I started towards the higher range to the left of camp. My intention was to try the ground straight ahead over the Nam Daba Pass. On my way, Taba pointed out to me a couple of rams, three or four hundred yards in front of us, of which one was a fine old fellow, whilst the other, a smaller, seemed to be wounded. Creeping up to within 150 yards I took my shot at the smaller animal and ended his sufferings. As this was close to the ground where my wife was shooting the previous day I accordingly sent my second man with the head and meat back to camp with the unexpected tidings. We turned westwards of the pass and presently spied five rams standing on a patch of snow, half way up a stony nullah.

[At this point Littledale left Demidoff to hunt his own bunch alone. Demidoff returned to camp at dusk.]

The ladies told me on my return that Littledale had sent in, through his second Kalmuk, a note which he had scribbled down on a flat bit of stone with flint . . . with the following words: "Wounded big sheep; send small tent and stores." This was indeed good news. The ladies had ordered the Kalmuk back with the necessary things for a night out.

On the following morning, there being no sign of Littledale, I sent Taba out in the hope that he might find some clue to the whereabouts of my wounded sheep, while I remained in camp in eager expectation. At 4 P.M. Taba returned, after an unsuccessful search. Half an hour later we perceived a small party riding towards us; this was Littledale with his two men. He brought in the finest head of *Ovis ammon* that had as yet been obtained, and it proved

116

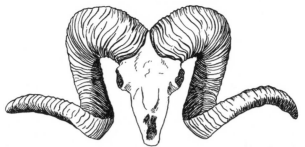

After Demidoff (1900)

This world's record Ammon head was taken by St. George Littledale in the Altai Mountains, on the Siberian-Mongolian border, in June, 1900. Measurements: H.L. 61½"; H.B.C. 20½"; H.T. 37½".

Even though this exceptionally fine specimen was taken more than sixty years ago, it still stands as the all-time record for all sheep heads. There now seems very little chance of its ever being surpassed, for these Ammon, like all wild sheep, have since suffered great depletion, while natives, now possessing high-powered rifles, are steadily reducing the few that still struggle for survival.

to be the record. Its measurements, as taken on the spot, were the following: Length, 63 inches; girth, 19½ inches; from tip to tip, 41½ inches. He gave us a most graphic account of his two days' experiences. He had come across the same herd which my wife had saluted with five shots from his "Mannlicher," and to which herd belonged the young ram I had finished off for her. He had waited a considerable time before the animals fed into stalkable ground, taking the utmost precaution not to miss the chance of securing the magnificent old ram he had "spotted" with his glass. Having got above them, the whole herd passed below him, and as the large one came up broadside-on, he had fired twice, shattering his hind quarters; but this, he found was not sufficient to stop him, and as he had only been able to take his shot late in the afternoon, he had decided to spend the night out, and follow him early the next day. The last he had seen of him at dusk, much to his discomfiture, was that, after having lain down several times, he had finally risen and walked slowly over a ridge. Next morning, at dawn, he was found lying some hundreds of yards below the ridge in the next corrie, still alive. He had to stalk him again, and put another bullet into him before he could secure him. . . . such is the vitality of these animals that only a mortal wound will stop them.

The Tibetan Argali

Ovis ammon hodgsoni

Courtesy of Mrs. William J. Morden

This Tibetan Argali is a ten-year-old *hodgsoni* taken by the late William J. Morden near Nyan, Rupshu, on the Tibetan-Indian border. The white neck and shoulder and something of the white bib may be seen behind the horns.

LET US LEAVE these northernmost *ammon* for a while and take an imaginary trip by plane southward within the Great Arc and head a little east-of-south for some 1,600 miles or more. We leave the Altai to fly first over the great Dzungarian Plateau, then top the twenty-thousand-foot Tien Shan system to pick up and cross the Taklamakan Desert, where we see the great range of the Karakoram in the far distance. Topping this and just ahead is the main range of the Himalayas, and we soon glide to the best field in extreme western Tibet along the border of India. We are now back where we left the Ladak Urials hobnobbing with the Tibetan Ammons.

From the Mediterranean up to this point our sheep have moved

Courtesy of H. T. Cowling

This view of the home of the Tibetan Argalis looks north from the borderland of northeastern India into Tibet, from an elevation of about 18,000 feet. These huge, sweeping, grassy slopes are typical of most of the sheep grounds of the Central Asian Argalis. The late William J. Morden is at left with the gun; H. T. Cowling stands beside the camera.

eastward, sometimes loosely attached and at other times in closely compressed continuity. Now, however, they divide into two great in-curved arms, with their pivotal point in the Poli country of the Russian Pamirs. The upper or northern arm, which we have just followed through to the *ammon* of the Altai, continues onward to the eastern end of the Argali's range; but the lower or southern arm, somewhat shorter yet still very long, curves downward and eastward through southern Tibet, across the high Tibetan Plateau, eastward through Bhutan and Sikkim, and northward along the Chinese border to the southern Gobi—in all a distance of some two thousand miles. This rather narrow but tremendous sweep of country is the exclusive range of one race of wild sheep, *Ovis ammon hodgsoni.* And this poses an interesting question—why? Why in all this vast region is there but one kind of *ammon*, when in the northern arm there is such a congestion of subspecies that they frequently overlap?

We may find our answer in the accessibility of the northern arm to hunters and scientists from Russia, and the Near Eastern trade routes on the west and India on the south, while the southern arm is protected by the great Himalayas to the south and the vastness of China to the north. Only now, with planes and modern equipment, is it possible even to consider penetrating this heretofore forbidden and foreboding land. And it may be that while scientists have described but one subspecies of *ammon* (*hodgsoni*) from this huge area, once they have gained access to the hinterland to study its fauna, they may discover other variations of this somewhat unique *ammon*. It seems very improbable that a sheep or any other animal would remain static in evolutionary development throughout an extended range of two thousand miles or more.

A Tibetan Argali (*hodgsoni*) head

The data on the *hodgsoni* head (A.M.N.H., No. 117571) shown in the above photographs are as follows: twelve-year-old ram; H.L. 41½"; H.B.C. 16½"; H.T. 22"; Sk. L. 14". Lydekker gives the world's record horns as: H.L. 57"; H.B.C. 18¾"; H.T. 29".

The Tibetan Argalis enjoy a very large and isolated range where there appears little or no chance of overlapping or intergradation with other subspecies of *ammon*.

Some say that they are the largest in body of all the Argalis, with a shoulder height of 48 to 52 inches, but the latter figure we may take with some reservation. Their horns are massive, compact, and comparatively tightly curled, sometimes hugging the cheeks very closely. The horns seldom exceed a complete circle. Their most characteristic feature is their white bib and neck which, unlike other Argalis, they are said to carry throughout the year. Their ears are very small, perhaps the smallest of all in this *ammon* group.

In color and color-pattern they vary somewhat from other Argalis, their body coat being a light tan-brown with sides and thighs darker. In winter these darker tones are said to turn to more of a grayish-brown. The muzzle, neck, rump-patch, under parts, and legs are rather conspicuously white.

Their favored habitat is the open, rolling plateau territory, from twelve to fifteen thousand feet in elevation. The most accessible hunting ground for sportsmen in search of this Argali is along the Kashmir-Tibetan border near Nian-Tsaga, where the Tibetans call him "Nyan."

Major Gerald Burrard, in his book *Big Game Hunting in the Himalayas and Tibet*, has good information on *hodgsoni*: "This magnificent creature essentially belongs to open, undulating country, rather than to precipitous mountains; and the flat plains, tilted levels and round-topped hills of Tibet form its home.... The chief point which impressed me when I first saw *Ammon* [*hodgsoni*] was their wonderful length of leg, compared with such animals as burrel, thar, ibex, or shapu. They seem built for galloping over open country, and without doubt the best places in which to find them are vast open spaces interspersed with hills in which there are valleys to provide shelter from both sun and wind when they lie up during the heat of the day.... As soon as the mean elevation of the country falls much below 14,000 feet *Ammon* are no longer found....

"*Ammon* are big animals standing quite twelve hands [48 inches] at the shoulders.... The average weight of a full-grown ram would probably be somewhere in the neighborhood of 210 to 220 lb....

"The colour is a very light brown with darker withers.... Full-grown rams develop a white ruff or mane, and in the distance they can be easily distinguished by the light colour of their heads and necks, for the horns, in spite of their great size, are light in colour and very difficult to see."

Evidently the Nyan's head and neck are very white, like those of a bull caribou, of which the saying goes, "The whiter the neck, the older the bull," indicating therefore larger horns.

The Altyn Argali

Ovis ammon dalai-lamae

A RARE SHEEP closely related to *Ovis ammon hodgsoni*, this Argali ranges the Altyn Tagh Mountains bordering the southern fringe of the Taklamakan Desert of south-central Sinkiang and the smaller adjoining Moscow and Columbus ranges to the south along the northeastern border of Tibet.

Little is known about this sheep, for it is rather isolated from all other Argalis except at the western limits of *hodgsoni*.

Francis Harper's data in *Extinct and Vanishing Mammals of the Old World* is "derived chiefly from Nasonov" and includes a citation from Przhevalsk (1888) reading: "Horn small, 32½ inches in length on the front curve; throat-ruff weakly developed, not clear white; muzzle, belly, groin and buttocks white; height at shoulder almost 4 feet."

And now, since there are no other Argalis to be considered this far south, we will "fly" back to the Altai to resume our journey eastward. We should, however, delay our departure long enough to review the case of two aberrant creatures (one conveniently near at hand), which look like true sheep but are not—that is, they are "sheep" from the sportsman's standpoint but not recognized as such by mammologists. One is called the Bharal or Blue sheep and the other the Aoudad or Barbary sheep.

The Bharal or Blue Sheep

Pseudois nayaur

Courtesy of the New York Zoological Society

A young Bharal or Blue sheep ram

FIRST CLASSIFIED as one of the true sheep (*Ovis*), it has since been given the status of a genus by itself. It is represented by its type (*Pseudois nayaur*) from western Tibet and a single subspecies (*Pseudois nayaur szechuanensis*) from the distant eastern end of its range along the western borderland of China.

Having certain characteristics of both the sheep (*Ovis*) and the goat (*Capra*), it is one of those deviations of nature which are not infrequent in evolutionary processes. Its swept-back horns are more goatlike than the spiraling horns of the sheep, but the characteristic beard of the goat is entirely lacking. The ears are long and the legs are shorter and stockier than those of sheep. The tail is said to be considerably longer than those of *Ovis*. The neck carries no throat-ruff or mane. Weighing around 150 pounds and standing about 36 inches at the shoulders, it ranges practically the whole of the open Tibetan Plateau upward of 10,000 feet. To the west its range extends into northern India as far as Leh, in Ladakh. In the east it follows the mountain ranges of the Tibetan-Szechwan

These two photographs of a fine fourteen-year-old ram in the N.C.H.H. show an exceptionally good specimen with characteristic swept-back horns. Said to have been taken near the Tibetan border in northern India, its measurements are as follows: H.L. 27½″; H.B.C. 10½″; H.T. 27″.

border northward as far as the Chinese province of Shensi. Although it frequents the grassy slopes, it is often encountered on precipitous cliffs.

It is a colorful sheep of a bluish-gray-brown, with whitish under parts and lower legs and a blackish marking along the front of the face, neck, and fore parts of legs. A blackish stripe runs along the body from elbow to flank, dividing the upper body-color from the abdominal white. Their much lighter winter coats are said to appear almost white when seen against a darker background.

The best recording of their horn length is 33½ inches. The next best, recorded by Rowland Ward in *Records of Big Game*, is: H.L. 31½″; H.B.C. 13½″; H.T. 22½″.

The horns are of a dark-olive color and quite smooth. Only the year-rings are noticeable and especially so when the insignificant corrugations become worn down, as they usually do in fully matured rams.

The Aoudad or Barbary Sheep

Ammotragus lervia

Courtesy of the New York Zoological Society

THIS INTERMEDIATE between the sheep and the goat has certain fundamentals different enough to cause it to be classified in a genus by itself. Similar to this genus in deviation is the goat-antelope group, which includes the Serow, Goral, and Takin of Asia, the Chamois of Europe, and the White Mountain goat of the Canadian Rockies.

If we consider the Aoudad to be a "sheep," then it is the only one transgressing the sheep's Great Arc, for it inhabits the arid hills and mountains of practically all of the Sahara region from the Atlantic to the Red Sea, southward as far as Khartoum, Kordofan, and the great bend of the Niger. Francis Harper states that it is also reported as formerly occurring in Palestine. It is now perhaps most plentiful in the countries bordering the Mediterranean Sea, particularly in Algeria.

Sometimes called "Udad" and "Arui," it is a rather large "sheep," from 36 to 39 inches at the shoulders, with definitely swept-back horns and a conspicuous, pendant mane of very long, straight hair hanging from the front of the neck, across the lower part of the shoulders, and around the upper part of the fore legs. Distinctive also is the long, tufted tail, which reaches to the vicinity of the hocks. Its color is a uniform light brick-red, with the mane somewhat darker in hue. The under-body parts are but slightly lighter than the upper-body tone. The horns carry very fine corrugations and become quite smooth with little wear. Rowland Ward gives the best head (from Algeria) as: H.L. 33¼"; H.B.C. 13¼"; H.T. 12½".

The direction of horn growth is similar to that of the swept-back horns of the Urials, which converge inwardly at the tips.

The suborbital face glands and the foot glands of the true sheep are lacking in this group, which carries some four subspecies dispersed throughout the Sahara region.

The Mongolian Argali
Ovis ammon darwini

Now RETURNING to the Altai Mountains, we leave our big *ammon* and look eastward across Mongolia and its rolling Gobi Desert Plateau, studded with low ranges and their outlying hills.

Throughout this arid land *ammon* are still to be found, but they are few and far between. Widely dispersed, they are limited to areas of good grazing—and good it must be, to build and sustain such sturdy bodies and big horns. There have been several subspecies of *ammon* described from this vast area, e.g., *mongolica*, *przevalskii*, *kozlovi*, *jubata*, *comosa*, etc., but gradually all these have been reclassified and are currently placed in *Ovis ammon darwini*, which now serves as the one subspecies for all forms of *ammon* throughout Mongolia.

A Mongolian Argali (*Ovis ammon darwini*)

The twelve-year-old *darwini* (A.M.N.H., No. 45491) shown above came from the Kwei-Hua-Chen Mountains, on the border of Mongolia and Shansi Province of north China. It was taken by Roy Chapman Andrews at about the five- to six-thousand-foot elevation on the high, rolling plateau country where the mountains themselves do not run very high.

Measurements: H.L. 46"; H.B.C. 18"; H.T. 29"; Sk. L. 13¾". While *darwini* horns do not extend their horn length to any great degree, they are said to grow the largest horn base of all sheep. I have heard of the recording of a base circumference of twenty-two inches. These pictures will also show the very heavy corrugation and the close curl of the horn (outer circle diameter). For some reason the horns are very dark in color, far darker than those of the Poli group at the western end of the Argali's range. It will also be noted that these horns rank their bearers among the "high-brows," perhaps the highest of all.

Ovis ammon darwini is one of the largest of the Argalis and is closely related to the *Ovis ammon ammon* and *Ovis ammon hodgsoni*. Arthur de Carle Sowerby, in *Sport and Science on the Sino-Mongolian Frontier*, gives their weight at 300 pounds for the male and 200 pounds for a female, which seems conservative for the male but about in line for the female, the latter being always considerably lighter, with their small horns a negligible factor in their over-all weight. Andrews describes this ram as "washed with white on neck and shoulders." Sowerby also reports their pelage as a "thick coat of a dark, grey-slate color." But our best color description is supplied by Glover M. Allen, in *The Mammals of China and Mongolia*: ". . . muzzle, sides of head and upper throat grayish brown slightly grizzled with white; rest of upper neck and the back yellowish brown, with a somewhat variegated or 'watered' appearance, varying from about 'sayal-brown' to 'snuff-brown'; flanks from axilla [armpit] to groin and front of thigh a more uniform and darker brown, nearly bistre; buttocks grading into 'light ochraceous buff' without a well-defined rump patch; tail with a brown medium line, buff sides and a number of white terminal hairs. Legs with a stripe down the front of mixed brown and white, the rest pale ochraceous buff. Belly whitish in the inguinal [groin] region, this pale area extending forward to the chest, where it becomes tinged with buff. Longest hairs on upper neck about 40 mm. [1½"], on the body about 20 mm. [¾"] long. Another skin from the same place has much more white.

"Skull length about 13⅞"; S.H. taken of 12 full-grown rams [ranges from] 41½" to 45½"; H.L. 47½" [maximum about 50"]. Horns do not attain the length of those of *O. ammon* [*Ovis ammon ammon*] but exceed them in girth. Horn tips are less everted. Skull greatest length 335 mm. [13¼"]."

Roy Chapman Andrews Hunts the Mongolian Argali

About four years after I entered The American Museum, Director Bumpus brought a young man into my studios and introduced
him, saying: "Clark, I want you to take care of this young fellow
and give him a place to work. Just what he will do I'm not sure but
I'll find something for him soon."

This young man was no less than the famous late Roy Chapman
Andrews. Being of about the same age, we became very good
friends—a friendship that lasted for over fifty years.

Roy had just graduated from Beloit College in Wisconsin and,
being a real outdoor man, had picked the American Museum for
his career. And thus it was that we both started out at the same time
to be "great and good" museum men—Roy becoming great while
I became good! Then one day Bumpus called me into his office.
A notice in the morning paper reported that a sixty-five-foot right
whale and her thirty-foot baby had just been harpooned off the
eastern end of Long Island by the local commercial fishermen.
They had been towed ashore and were about to be cut up and
rendered for the oil, while the valuable whalebone was to be sold
commercially.

Director Bumpas said: "Clark, I want you to go up there at once,
buy those two whales from the fishermen, and save their complete
skeletons and whalebone as specimens for the Museum. And I'll
authorize you to pay them $2,500 for the two." Then he added:
"You will give them all the blubber, which is really what they
want, for their labor in cutting out the bones and whalebone.
Now," he went on, "this is a big job and you will probably want
to take someone along with you. Whom would you want?" There
was no question in my mind who this "someone" would be and I
immediately replied, "I think I'll take this young fellow Andrews.
He's a good live-wire!"

And so it was that Andrews and I went on our very first Museum
expedition together.

In the years that followed we both made many expeditions in
behalf of the Museum. But while fate took me eastward into Africa,
Roy went westward to the Pacific to follow up his study of whales

and into China and Mongolia to explore for fossils, where he eventually discovered, among many other important specimens, the famous dinosaur eggs. Knowing of Roy's experience in hunting the Mongolian Argalis, I read his books and wrote him letters, to which he generously replied—and with his permission I here quote the story of one of his Mongolian Argali hunts, from his book *Across Mongolian Plains*:

"A Mongolian Argali Hunt"

THE HUNTING GROUNDS were five days' travel from Pekin. Brigands always had to be considered [but] there are many sheep there. They are the last survivors of great herds which once roamed the mountains of No. China. In size as well as ancestry the members of this group are the grandfathers of all the sheep. The largest ram of our Rocky Mountains is a pygmy compared with a full-grown Argali. Hundreds of thousands of years ago the big-horns, which

Courtesy of The American Museum of Natural History
Roy Chapman Andrews with a fine Mongolian Argali

originated in Asia, crossed into Alaska by way of the Bering Sea, where there was probably a land connection at that time. From Alaska they gradually worked southward, along the mountains of the western coast, into Mexico and lower California. In the course of time changed environment developed different species; but the migration route from the Old World to the New is there for all to read."

[And then Andrews, describing something of the country and

people, passes through the last outpost, Kwei-Hua-Chen, not far from the sheep ground:]

Fifteen hundred feet above us towered a ragged granite ridge which must be crossed ere we could gain entrance to the grassy valley beyond the barrier. We toiled halfway up the slope, when my hunter sank into the grass, pointed ahead and whispered "pan-yang" (wild sheep). There on the very summit of the highest pinnacle, stood a magnificent ram silhouetted against the sky. . . . Through my glasses I could see every detail of its splendid body—the wash of grey with which many winters had tinged its neck and flanks, the finely drawn legs and the massive horns curling about the head as proudly held as that of a Roman warrior. He stood like a statue for half an hour, while we crouched motionless in the trail below; then he turned deliberately and disappeared.

When we reached the summit of the ridge the ram was nowhere to be seen but we found his tracks on a path leading down a knife-like outcrop to the bottom of another valley. . . . I was just tearing the wrapper from a piece of chocolate when the [i.e., my] hunter touched me on the arm and said quietly, "pan-yang li la" (a sheep has come). He pointed far down the ridge running out at the right . . . [and there he stood]. For an hour we watched him. Sometimes he would turn about to look across the ravines and once he came a dozen feet towards us. I must confess that I had little hope. The ram seemed too splendid and much, much too far away. A flock of red-legged partridges sailed across from the opposite ridge.

When I looked at the sheep again he was lying down squarely on the trail lazily raising his head now and then to gaze about. . . . We rolled slowly over the ridge and then hurried around to a projecting spur at the end of which the ram was lying. . . . Pushing my rifle over the rocks before me, I raised myself a few inches and saw the massive head and neck of the ram two hundred yards away. His body was behind a rocky shoulder, but he was looking squarely at us and in a second would be off. I aimed carefully just under his chin, and at the roar of the high-powered shell, the ram leaped backwards. . . . When we finally descended the animal lay halfway down the slope, feebly kicking. What a huge brute he was, and what a glorious head. I had never dreamed that an Argali could be so splendid. His horns were perfect and my hands could not meet around them at the base.

THE ASIATIC BIGHORNS

Ovis nivicola

LEAVING THE BIG ARGALIS in Mongolia, we now follow the sheep's Great Arc as it swings northeasterly up through central and eastern Siberia, where we come upon another interesting sheep, which until recently was classified as a subspecies of the American Bighorn.

This classification, in *canadensis*, was mainly due to the fact that the sheep carried the rounder horn of the American Bighorn and not the triangular horn of the Argali group. Although now re-classified as a separate species, *Ovis nivicola* (snow-inhabiting) are still colloquially called the Asiatic Bighorns.[1]

The distribution of this group, which encompasses the whole eastern half of Siberia, covers an area almost twice that of the Argali group.

In body size they are something less than the North American Bighorn (*Ovis canadensis canadensis*), nearer perhaps to that of the American Dall and the Desert sheep, which would be around 36 to 38 inches at the shoulders.

Their well-formed, spiraling horns are smaller in horn-circle diameter, less massive, and quite smooth, with a prominent "keel" or ridge around the outer edge. The heavy and shaggy, woollike coat is somewhat different in coloring and pattern from that of the average sheep pelage, some carrying a considerable amount of white on the head and shoulders, as does the male Stone sheep in his later years. Basically, the coloring and color-pattern of *Ovis nivicola* is a grayish, grizzly-brown with a more predominantly grayish tone extending up the neck and over the face. Their one distinctive marking is the wide, darkish-brown band running across

[1] For the classification listing of the Asiatic Bighorn group, see Appendix IV.

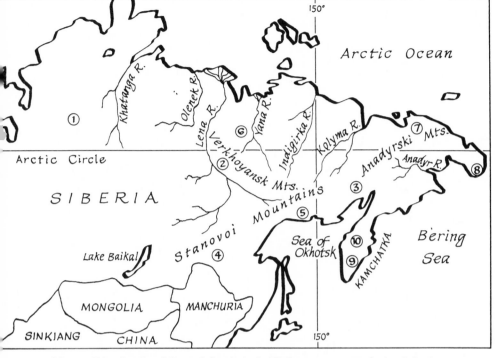

Map 4. Distribution Map of the Asiatic Bighorns. 1, 2, 3, *Ovis nivicola borealis*; 4, *Ovis nivicola potanini*; 5, *Ovis nivicola alleni*; 6, *Ovis nivicola lydekkeri*; 7, 8, 9, 10, *Ovis nivicola nivicola*.

the face between eyes and nose to the lower half of each cheek. The rear edges of the front and hind legs carry the usual whitish trim, while the frontal areas of the legs are of a rich, dark brown. The white rump-patch is small, terminating more or less at the base of the tail. The under parts are of the usual whitish color. But, as with the Urials, we can expect much of this coloration to vary considerably in its several widely dispersed subspecies.

These color-patterns appear to be more prominent in the *nivicola* of western Sibera, while those of the eastern coastal areas have lost many of these markings to a more uniform grayish-brown. They are said to have a broad muzzle, very short ears, and a short, broad skull, carrying pronounced orbital borders indicating a long or heavily haired pelage. Several over-all skull measurements, taken

137

by the author, averaged about 10¼ inches, with the largest measuring 10¾ inches. According to Richard Lydekker, in *Wild Oxen, Sheep, and Goats of All Lands*, "a full-grown [Kamchatka] ram, in good condition, will weigh about 330 lbs."

Based on the maximum weight given for an *Ovis canadensis canadensis*, (344 pounds), which is a much larger sheep (42 inches at the shoulders) with far more massive and heavier horns, Lydekker's estimate of 330 pounds seems far in excess of the actual weight. It is my considered opinion that 230 pounds or at most 250 pounds would be a generous weight for any Asiatic Bighorn. I have found no horn-length measurements exceeding 41½ inches or horn-base circumference exceeding 14½ inches.

This Asiatic Bighorn group is represented by the species type *Ovis nivicola nivicola*, and by four subspecies.

Although there are not too many available data on these remote and widely scattered sheep, many specimens are known to exist, and there is doubtless much information on them behind the Iron Curtain in the Zoological Museum of the Russian Academy of Sciences at Leningrad. However, as this is not easily available and almost all of the scientific papers on the subject are in Russian, we shall have to consider them with whatever information is at hand.

Ian McTaggart Cowan contributes a highly interesting statement regarding them in his article "Distribution and Variation in the Native Sheep of North America," *American Midland Naturalist* (November, 1940): "*Ovis nivicola* of northeastern Asia, while possessing specific characters of its own, is more closely related to the North American Sheep than are any of the other Asiatic species and probably represents the Asiatic descendants of a sheep ancestral to those of North America."

Thus, having first established themselves in America, they could have drifted back into Asia during the long glacial periods, which could account for their close relationship to the American sheep.

The Syverma Bighorn

Ovis nivicola borealis

THIS MOST WESTERN Asiatic Bighorn (see Map 4, No. 1) ranges the region of the Syverma Mountains, between the sources of the Piasina and Khatanga rivers of north-central Siberia.

It is thought by some to be the intermediate between the *ammon* and the more eastern *nivicola* groups. However, it appears to be much closer to the latter because of its smaller body and horns.

Map 4, No. 2, shows another locality for *borealis*, ranging the Verkhoyansk Mountains along the upper reaches of the Lena River in central Siberia. This sheep is said to be "a small, darkish-brown sheep with a slight suggestion of a bib." One horn measurement is given as: H.L. 37"; H.B.C. 11"; H.T. 22".

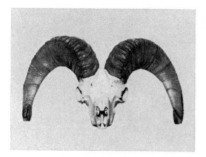

The Syverma Bighorn (*Ovis nivicola borealis*)

Here we have a good picture of a *borealis* head from the collection of the A.M.N.H. (No. 18212). This ten-year-old *borealis* ram was taken at the end of the Stanovoi Mountains (Map 4, No. 3) near Chichiga, a city at the northern end of the Gulf of Shelekhov. These three far-flung locality records for *borealis*, if valid, point to a remarkaby extended range for any single subspecies of sheep.

Horn measurements of the head shown above are: H.L. 29½"; H.T. 18".

The photographs will also show the high pitch at which the

horns rise from the skull and the Asiatic Bighorn's very small horn-circle diameter. It will be noted that the side view of the head reflects the sickle-shaped horns so characteristic of the Urial. This may have no significance, but if it holds true with all *nivicola*, it may reflect this species' horn characteristic.

Clifton's Bighorn
Ovis nivicola lydekkeri

After Lydekker (1913)

CLIFTON'S BIGHORN (Map 4, No. 6) ranges above the Arctic Circle in north-central Siberia between the Lena and Yana rivers. It is said to have an extensive distribution and to be quite plentiful.

Francis Harper quotes Richard Lydekker as follows in *Extinct and Vanishing Mammals of the Old World*: "Essentially the same type of animal (as the Kamchatka Bighorn (*O. n. nivicola*)) although its coloration is decidedly lighter, there is a much greater proportion of white, and the dorsal streak and tail are much darker. . . . In the male . . . the white rump-patch is much larger. . . . The face, too, is white, with the exception of a wood-brown transverse band midway between the nostrils and the eyes, which expands out-ward to include each cheek. The whole nape is also white mingled with grey. An indistinct dark line runs down the back and becomes more distinct as it approaches the tail, which is black-ish brown. There is also a larger proportion of white on the legs and under parts. . . . A female head . . . is wholly greyish white, passing into pure white on the forehead and muzzle."

This description gives us a vivid picture of quite a colorful sheep carrying considerable white, punctuated with splashes of brown.

Yablonov Bighorn

Ovis nivicola potanini

THIS ASIATIC BIGHORN ranges the Yablonovy and Stanovoi Mountains (Map 4, No. 4) of south-central Siberia, just north of Manchukuo. According to Francis Harper, in *Extinct and Vanishing Mammals of the Old World*, "practically all the information on this sheep, including the original description, is sequestered in the Russian literature."

So we have no alternative but to assume that it is perhaps little different from the rest of these *nivicola* sheep.

Allen's Bighorn
Ovis nivicola alleni

EXCEPT THAT this particular sheep is found in parts of the Stanovoi Range (Map 4, No. 5) in southeastern Siberia, I have found little in the literature concerning it.

The type was described from skull and horns only, showing the horns slightly more divergent than those of the species type (*Ovis nivicola nivicola*). Their horn circle was described as "less complete." The horn measurements are cited by Francis Harper, in *Extinct and Vanishing Mammals of the Old World*, as: H.L. 28¾"; H.T. 17⅞".

The Kamchatka Bighorn

Ovis nivicola nivicola (a form of *storcki*)

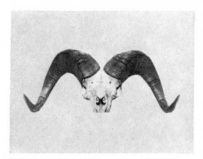 

This seven-year-old *nivicola* was taken on the Kamchatka Peninsula, not far from where the type specimen of *nivicola* was secured. It shows a young ram at the halfway mark of its life expectancy, which would be from fourteen to fifteen years. Measurements of this head are: H.L. (right) 30½"; H.L. (left) 30½"; H.B.C. (right) 13¾"; H.B.C. (left) 13¾"; H.T. 25¾"; Sk. L. 10¾".

THIS KAMCHATKA BIGHORN, the species type (Map 4, Nos. 7, 8, 9, and 10), ranges the extreme eastern area of Siberia. Although the four numbers spot the same species, they are here presented to show where specimens of *nivicola* have definitely been taken with accompanying data that may generally apply to the rest of this *nivicola* group. Data given on this sheep: Wt. 200 lbs.; S.H. 36–38"; H.L. 39"; H.B.C. 14"; H.T. 28"—all of which reflects a good-sized sheep.

On Map 4, No. 7 spots the extreme northern range of this group in the Anadyrski Mountains, running across the Arctic Circle.

Number 8 on the map gives us another *nivicola* record from the very tip of eastern Siberia. Exactly what sheep it is, we do not yet know, for this one specimen (now said to be in the National Museum, Washington) offers insufficient evidence for a conclusive answer. But because of its locality we can assume it to be none other than *Ovis nivicola nivicola*, since no other *nivicola* race has been found this far east. Although it is a female, it establishes an eastern limit for *nivicola*.

This specimen was taken in the midsummer of 1921 by John B. Burnham, of Essex, New York, on the Chukotski Peninsula. It was an adult female, on which Burnham gives the following data in *The Rim of Mystery*: "Color ... warm mouse-gray like a caribou's summer coat. ... Estimated weight 110 lbs. ... H.L. 10½"; H.T. 17½". These horn measurements reflect an extraordinarily wide spread for horns of that length, but this could well be an individual variation rather than a fixed horn character.

The world's record Kamchatka Bighorn

The Kamchatka Bighorns are said to carry a pelage quite different in texture from that of their American cousins, their coats being of a thick, woollike hair of a grayish-brown or grizzled color and in winter very long and shaggy. The rump-patch, which is rather small, is divided by a conspicuous dark stripe continuing down a dark and bushy tail. The legs carry the usual white trim. The muzzle is white but the dark, wood-brown face-band of the Clifton sheep is now almost lost. There is a tendency for the head and neck to carry a tinge of grayish-white that sometimes becomes quite noticeable. Specimens with their heads and necks almost a pure white are reported to be in the Tring Park Museum, Tring, Hertfordshire, England. This is interesting, for we sometimes find the closely related Stone sheep carrying white heads and necks. This of course may be due to seasonal change or age, but it might have significance as a possible answer to the question of how the White Dall sheep happened to become all white.

The Kamchatka Bighorn pictured above (A.M.N.H., No.

22689) is the type specimen for all the Siberian Bighorns. Taken at Fort Tigil in the east-central section of the Kamchatka Peninsula (Map 4, No. 10), it was first described by Dr. J. A. Allen, of the A.M.N.H., in 1901.

It is the oldest sheep head (fourteen years), that I have ever handled or know of and must certainly be a world's record for the Asiatic Bighorn group, for with its very considerable age, perfect tips, and over-all symmetry, it would be difficult to match. Even though the Chadwick world's record Stone sheep (see below) is considered by many to be the finest of the fine among North American big-game trophies in any class, this little Asiatic Bighorn, I believe, surpasses it.

With a horn-circle diameter of only ten inches, it carries a curl just short of one and one-half turns. But perhaps its most extraordinary feature is the delicacy of the horn tips, which end as sharp as the point of a woman's little finger. And while the year-rings prove that it is a fourteen-year-old ram, the horns and skull weigh but 15 pounds.

George H. Storck, who collected this specimen, wrote: "Specimens of this sheep are very hard to get, as they are found only in the central range of mountains in the northwestern portion of Kamchatka; and it is the most difficult place to travel in, that I have ever faced, both on account of the roughness of the country and the almost constant storms that rage all through the winter, which is practically the only season when one can travel in the interior."[1]

We are fortunate in having an excellent description of these sheep from F. H. H. Guillemard, who was the medico-member of a Russian expedition to Kamchatka in 1885. He reported on these sheep in the *Proceedings of the Zoological Society of London* (1885), as follows: ". . . near volcanoes, lower part of great Kamchatka River, Russia, shot several on sea cliffs of the east coast some 50 miles E. NE. of Petropaulovsky. . . . Returning from Bering Island we could see small herds on the slopes of cliffs which rose to 500–600 feet. In two days obtained 13 specimens—all full grown males. . . . *Color*—brownish-grey [Sept.] with hair long and

[1] In J. A. Allen, *A New Sheep from Kamchatka.*

thick. Head and neck more distinctly grey than rest of body. Fore-head with an ill-marked darker patch; upper and under lips greyish white. Anterior aspect of limbs, dark, glossy brown; a line down posterior, aspect white. Tail short, dark-brown, center of belly and rump white; this color does not surround the tail. Ears re-markably short."

From a fine series of measurements recorded by Guillemard from the thirteen specimens mentioned, I have deduced the follow-ing: S.H.: Although Dr. Guillemard recorded three adult speci-mens at 40", 40½", and 41" respectively, the average shoulder height of the eleven males measured by him is around 39". These, then, are not small sheep at all, probably somewhere between the size of the *dalli* and the *canadensis* Bighorn. Wt.: average (big males) around 225–50 lbs. H.L. average around 35–38", with a probable maximum of 41½", as in the "type" specimen. H.B.C. 13–14", with a probable maximum of 14½". H.T. 20–25", with a maximum of 28". Sk. L. 10½", with a probable maximum of 11".

By a relative comparison with other sheep data on shoulder height and skull length relation, it would seem that, the skull length being a fixed norm, the shoulder heights as given by Guillemard are in excess of this relationship.

It is possible that Guillemard measured these shoulder heights with the front leg extended rather than with the leg and shoulder in to the position which they would normally assume when the animal was standing. This could make a minus difference of two to four inches, bringing this height–skull-length relationship into a more realistic balance. As it now stands we have a sheep with its head apparently too small for its body. But what seems remarkable is that of the four or five *nivicola* heads which I have examined, not one has a suggestion of a damaged horn tip. Especially when their habitat is, as Storck says, "the most difficult place to travel in, that I have ever faced . . . on account of roughness" and, as Guillemard notes, "small herds [are] on the slopes of cliffs which rose to 500–600 feet," is seems incredible that the sheep could keep their horn tips so perfect. At least it is evident that they must be passive crea-tures and not aggressive fighters. And all these races of Asiatic

Bighorns appear to be mountain dwellers, according to the localities named, which are invariably mountain ranges.

In 1899, Prince Demidoff and St. George Littledale spent the summer hunting these *nivicola* in the shadow of the eight-thousand-foot extinct volcano of Kamchatkaia Vershina in south-central Kamchatka. They were in virgin country where, their old guide told them, no white man or native, except himself, had ever been.

They hunted the large open valleys ranging from three to five thousand feet, while higher, extinct volcanoes were not infrequent. The ground was rough and rugged with much volcanic rock, all too often making for very hard going. Sheep were everywhere and so were bears. Hardly a day passed without their seeing from one to six bears, which were probably a form of grizzly. Demidoff tells of having on one occasion six of these bears in the field of his glasses at one time, lying on a big snowfield, apparently to keep cool and escape the mosquitoes, which were "in great abundance."

In *A Shooting Trip to Kamchatka*, Demidoff gives some very good firsthand information on these Kamchatka sheep: "*Ovis nivicola* is considerably more plentiful along the [eastern] coast, where life is made easier both on account of the constant breeze which blows in winter, as well as capital grazing, partly due to the sea salt. During the two warm months they betake themselves to the highest ground [five thousand feet] and adopt the habits of wild goats, living in the tightest rocks."

He notes their pelage as: ". . . [Ram] coat uniform dark grey with lighter tinge on face, under belly and around legs. . . . Three year old sheep . . . her coat was a clean slaty-grey colour, with the usual light parts on rump, legs and belly."

He mentions seeing a " 'grey' spot moving among rocks," and again: ". . . one carried thick brown patches of winter hair . . . summer coat is of dull grey hue, lighter on legs, rump and under belly."

A black and white photograph in his book captioned "Ovis nivicola (an old ram)" shows a complete mounting in its short summer coat, which appears to be quite uniform in color and length of hair. It also shows a whitish muzzle, a whitish ring around the eyes, and ears that are whitish, at least on their fore part.

The legs are of the same darkish body-color clear to the hoofs except with a very narrow white trim running down the rear edges. The underbelly appears of the same body-color except for a narrow strip of white along the medial line of the abdomen. The black of the knees continues, although somewhat diminished, down the front of the fore legs to the ankles, which it then seems to encircle. Demidoff gives the shoulder height of a full-grown ram as forty inches and a weight of from 200 to 250 pounds.

This would make *nivicola* about the same in size as the Stone sheep, which is next in size to our Rocky Mountain Bighorn—or equal in size to the second-largest sheep in North America.

Of the ten or twelve rams which Demidoff and Littledale obtained the four best measured:

H.B.C.	H.L.
14½″	39″
14½″	38½″
14½″	35″
13½″	34″

Not a single head among all those which they obtained showed the least suggestion of a broomed tip. And particularly noticeable was the consistently slight divergence of the main beams in every head.

The shoulder measurement of forty inches is about in line with those noted by Guillemard, and while it is always helpful to have a record of data from someone "on the spot," we must take it with some reservation until it has been evaluated. In this case it appears that *nivicola* at 40 inches and *stonei* also at 40 inches are approximately equal in size. But their skull lengths do not reflect this, with *nivicola*'s skulls measuring around 10½ inches while *stonei*'s skulls measure around 12 inches. It would seem therefore that *nivicola* would be a smaller sheep than *stonei*, perhaps plus or minus 35 inches or about the size of the Urials, whose skull lengths also run around 10½ inches.

Demidoff and Guillemard may also have made the common mistake of extending the front leg to its greatest length before taking the measurement.

PART THREE

The Sheep of North America

THE SHEEP OF NORTH AMERICA

LEAVING THE EASTERN SHORES OF SIBERIA, the Great Arc of the Wild Sheep continues across the Bering Sea into North America via Alaska. From here it turns southward to encompass the Rocky Mountains and their coastal ranges as far south as northern Mexico and the peninsula of Lower California. Nowhere else in the Western Hemisphere are the wild sheep to be found.

There are but two species of wild sheep in America: *Ovis dalli* and *Ovis canadensis*. The *Ovis dalli* group is at home in most of Alaska, the southwestern Yukon, and extreme northwestern British Columbia, while *Ovis canadensis* loosely populates the coastal and main range of the Rockies from southern Alberta and British Columbia southward to northern Mexico and Lower California.

It is believed that American sheep are descendants of an early Asian stock that long ago drifted into North America by way of this Bering Sea land bridge.

The history of this "bridge" is roughly the history of the four great glacial periods which are loosely encompassed within the Pleistocene epoch that dates back 500,000 to 1,000,000 years.

Underlying Bering Sea between Siberia and Alaska is a very extensive plateau which Hopkins[1] calls the "Chuckchi-Bering Platform," which is "monotonously flat" and covered by relatively shallow water. This platform is said to carry few, if any, deep gorges and very few uplifts like that of Diomede Islands, and it is from this slightly submerged platform that the Bering Sea land bridge was believed to have risen.

[1] The author is indebted to David M. Hopkins for much factual information contained in his fine article, "Cenozoic History of the Bering Land Bridge," *Science* (June 5, 1959).

The theory is that at the maximum peak of each glacial period this land bridge, which was believed to have been intermittent, came into being only when the great icecaps, having captured so much moisture (water), lowered the sea by an estimated two to three hundred feet. Thus was exposed this higher portion of the ocean's floor which was to become the historic bridge. Conversely, during the warmer interglacial periods the glaciers melted to raise again the water level to its present status. Thus this temporary route of migration was completely submerged to where it now rests some two hundred feet below the surface of the sea.

It is known that there have been several of these land bridges throughout the world. Some have come into being by the uplift of the underlying land mass, through volcanic action or the lowering of the sea. Some of these shifts were major while others were minor, but all were no doubt factors which could have affected evolutionary trends in both men and animals. The Isthmus of Panama and Central America, once entirely under water, now form one of these major, living land bridges. And England had her land bridge connecting her to Continental Europe. But of all these bridges the Bering Sea land bridge was perhaps one of the most important, for it was undoubtedly alone responsible for populating the Western Hemisphere with the ancient, higher order of animals and men.

There is evidence that the Bering Sea land bridge was a low, treeless tundra of very considerable width, rich with grasses and quite free from glaciation. Glaciers, however, are said to have intruded on the near-by shore lines of Siberia and Alaska, and into the north-central parts of America and Siberia. But these glaciers were apparently small impediment to the immigrants who had the urge to move east or west. It is believed that Alaska was not heavily glaciated, which, if true, could have well encouraged many Asiatic mammals to settle and thrive there. This thought might well be substantiated by the many fossil and living animals which are to be found there today.

Some ten to eleven thousand years ago the fourth and last ice age began to wane, and the waters of its icecaps again lifted the sea to submerge this Bering land bridge. This last declining ice age is evidenced today by the presence of the many large glaciers and ice fields in and around Alaska. The great ice fields of the Mount St. Elias region are hundreds of square miles in area, and, in places, up to two thousand feet thick. And the great continent of Greenland still slumbers under her huge icecap, known to be ten thousand feet in depth in its central basin.

Conceding that the American sheep came to America by way of the now invisible Bering Sea land bridge, it seems probable that the first to come over were perhaps the progenitors of the Rocky Mountain Bighorns which, because of their not disimilar, massive horns, are thought to have stemmed from the "Bighorns" of Central Asia. Apparently they drifted through mildly glaciated Alaska and settled eventually in the northern Rockies.

Then came the glaciers to push them southward. But it is thought that the northern Bighorns were spared an oasis of green where they were able to subsist and survive these northern glacial periods while others (the so-called Desert sheep) continued southward, stopping just south of the border. With the recession of the glaciers some of them remained where they were while others drifted back northward. But apparently part of this northern migration followed the lower, more arid coastland and mountains of western North America and came to a halt in southern British Columbia. This would account for the fact that some of the present Desert sheep (*Ovis canadensis sierra* and *Ovis canadensis californiana*) have extended their present range so far northward.

THE DALL SHEEP

Ovis dalli

Alaskan White sheep group in the Academy of Natural Sciences, Philadelphia. This picture shows the White sheep's strong tendency toward flaring horns. Yet they also, and not infrequently, go to the other extreme of being tightly curled and nipped-in at the cheeks. While this picture shows horns with unimpaired tips, in many adults, especially those with the tight, close-cheek curl, the tips are heavily broomed.

IMMEDIATELY on reaching the mainland of Alaska we find in the middle of this otherwise unbroken chain of wild sheep a "pocket" or paradox, where a totally different group of sheep shows up with its type species and one subspecies all white, and its only other subspecies all black. What evolutionary process brought such a complete diversity of coloration poses some interesting questions.

155

T. Donald Carter, of The American Museum of Natural History, said, when I asked on what grounds the Dall sheep rated classification as a distinct species: "The Dall group have both teeth and horn differences great enough to warrant their separation from the *canadensis* group into a species by themselves."[1]

There are three races in this group: *Ovis dalli dalli*, the typical race; *Ovis dalli kenaiensis*, the Peninsula sheep; and *Ovis dalli stonei*, the Stone or Black sheep, the latter two being subspecies of *Ovis dalli dalli*. The first two are all white but are in no sense albinos, for they carry the characteristic golden eye of the Ovis family.

The Peace River, in its east-west course bisecting British Columbia, is a definite barrier that serves as a dividing line between the northern Dall group and the American Bighorns to the southeast. Although it may be possible for sheep to negotiate this river, especially in low water, there is no record of their having done so.

The Dall, especially in their white phase, seem to have greater variation in horn flare than any other sheep. They run from a tight, closely curled, converging head to a very widely extended, open spiral. Although the Stone (or Black) sheep sometimes carry these extreme variations, they are less prone to do so. *Ovis dalli kenaiensis*, on the other hand, which carries the smallest horns of the group, appears to keep closer to the normal. It is interesting to note that these flaring horns are seldom broomed, while those with the tight, close curl are invariably so.

Regarding the sizes and weights of these sheep I consulted Frank Dufresne, until recently chief of the Alaskan Game Commission at Juneau, Alaska, and quote from his reply: "I'd say a good big male [*Ovis dalli dalli*] will run around 180 lbs., occasionally a fat one would crowd 200. The Stone Sheep I've looked at all appeared to be a trifle larger than the White Dalls. Give them 200 for a big one, possibly 210 or even a few lbs. more for the exceptional fat ram. Of course lots of them will fall in the class between 180 and 200. Summing it up, average weight [of the Stone sheep is] 15 or 20 lbs. more than most of the Alaska White Sheep. If you want to

---

[1] For the classification listing of the Dall group, see Appendix V.

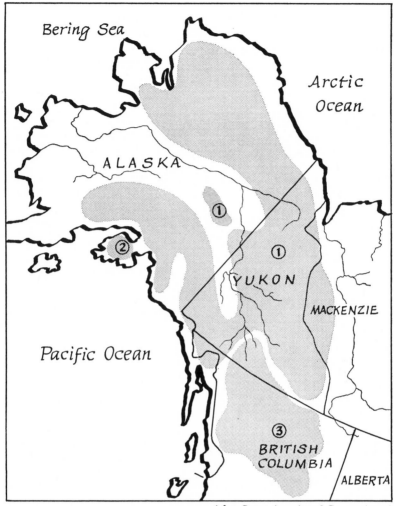

After Seton (1929) and Cowan (1940)

Map 5. Distribution Map of the *Ovis dalli*. 1, *Ovis dalli dalli*; 2, *Ovis dalli kenaiensis*; 3, *Ovis dalli stonei*.

include the rare, oversize 'lunker' you'd have to boost the maximum on White Sheep to 220 lbs. and the maximum on Stone Sheep to maybe 240."

Their horns are decidedly lighter in color than those of most other sheep except perhaps the Poli and its close relatives.

The marked difference in pelage coloration of the Dall and the Stone sheep may be explained by the likelihood of two separate migrations from Asia; or in the event of a single migration, by division after arrival in Alaska. In either case these two sheep, although of the same ancestral stock, must have been completely out of contact with each other for a very long time to undergo such a complete diversity of pelage color without intergradation.

Only in one small, single area where their ranges now come close together has any intergradation been reflected by a mixing of color. This area is the Pelly Mountains of the south-central Yukon, and this contact must have been of very recent date; otherwise we should find a far larger number similarly affected.

If the Asiatic Bighorns and Dall sheep are, as scientists say, closely related (and there is strong evidence in support of this), then we have some clue as to whence these Dall sheep got their white coats. Some of the *nivicola* group, as will be recalled, carry considerable white in their pelage.

The Alaskan White or Dall Sheep

Ovis dalli dalli

A good average White sheep from Alaska, in the N.C.H.H. The type specimen was described as from the mountains west of Fort Reliance, Alaska. This nine-and-one-half-year-old ram's head measures: H.L. 44"; H.B.C. 15"; H.T. 27½".

The Number Two world's record White sheep, now in the Academy of Natural Sciences, Philadelphia, measures: H.L. (right) 44½"; H.L. (left) 43¾"; H.B.C. (right) 14⅞"; H.B.C. (left) 14⅝"; H.T. 23½".

Ovis dalli was first described as *Ovis montana dalli* because it was thought to be a subspecies of the American Bighorn; however, its status as a subspecies has been reconsidered, and pertinent differences in the teeth and horns were sufficient to place it in a species by itself with the present name of *Ovis dalli*.

It is a slightly smaller sheep than the Bighorn, with the shoulder height for a big ram running from 38 to 40 inches.

This fine specimen of the Dall or White sheep was taken by F. Edmond-Blanc in Alaska, 1937, and mounted by the author. Its measurements are: H.L. 42⅝″; H.B.C. 14¾″; H.T. 21⅞″. While the picture shows the flaring type of horns, seemingly more common in this species than in any other sheep except the Poli, it is not uncommon to find an occasional White sheep with horns growing even closer to the cheeks than those shown here.

It is interesting to note that the horns, although not as large in base circumference, are not unlike those of the Tibetan Argali.

The Peninsula White Sheep
Ovis dalli kenaiensis

The *kenaiensis*, a subspecies of *Ovis dalli*, is a somewhat smaller, all-white sheep, with little difference except in size of body and horns, which seem to have little tendency to diverge or converge, holding closely to their characteristic parallel-beamed horn growth. The small horns, with their small horn-circle diameter, appear diminutive.

Their range is confined to the limits of the relatively small Kenai Peninsula on the south-central coast of Alaska. Here they inhabit the rich, grassy hills, blessed with a tempered climate from the Japan current. Although there is no effective natural barrier between this sheep and its larger cousin immediately to the north, except a very narrow, open area of lowland connecting the Peninsula to the mainland, there appears to be little or no intergradation between the two.

The horn measurements of the specimen shown above are: H.L. 34½"; H.B.C. 12½"; H.T. 18"; H.C.D. 11½". The skull length of one seven-year-old specimen measured 11½".

Charles Sheldon Hunts the Dalli

Charles Sheldon opens the Preface of his very good book, *The Wilderness of the Upper Yukon*, as follows: "This book is a record of my field experiences while engaged in studying the color variation of the wild sheep of the Yukon Territory. It is an attempt to give a detailed account strictly from the point of view of a hunter interested in natural history."

The particular region of this study was the Pelly Mountains in the southwestern portion of the Yukon, where the White and the Black *dalli* come together and interbreed. This interbreeding resulted in the *Ovis dalli fannini*, which William T. Hornaday described in 1901.

But at that time there was little known of these sheep or of the extent of their ranges. Thus Sheldon, as a real hunter and student of the sheep in general, went out to spend the winter in a small log cabin in an endeavor to solve some of these questions.

And now that we are considering this Dall group, I believe it appropriate to quote from one of Sheldon's many experiences, which well reflect his capacity not only as a sheep hunter and a lover of the grandeur of their mountainous habitats but also as a meticulous observer and a colorful raconteur:

JULY 28 (1905)—After hours of sleep I was awakened by the loud clucking of a ptarmigan close to my shelter and soon heard the peeping of the scattered chicks, which were hurriedly gathering around her. Several ground-squirrels, whose holes were very near the camp, were running about or sitting up and chattering. . . .

After lunch I started for the mountain south-east of camp, and in two and a half hours succeeded in reaching the crest. Looking through my field-glasses along the slopes of the rough mountain behind the camp, I could see seven sheep which were too distant to make out the sex. Proceeding along the crest I reached the highest peak, seven thousand five hundred and fifty feet in altitude. A sheep-trail followed the ridge-roof of the crest, and a few old tracks of ewes and lambs were there. I heard one cony, and saw two rock ptarmigan. Mists bringing light showers of rain, all gathering exclusively around the mountain on which I stood, continually floated by and enveloped me, while to the south-west the sky was clear, and I reached the head of the basin just as the sun was sinking.

Massed around the basin were gothic-spired ranges whose peaks fell in vertical cliffs many hundreds of feet to the steeply inclined talus which led to the soft, green pastures below. The serried crests, marbled with snow, burning with red, iron-stained rock, glowing with granites, caught the sunlight and were bathed in a rosy hue, while numerous little rainbows, formed in the spray of the small cataracts that dashed over the precipices, reflected their brilliant colors in contrast to the dark rocks and shadowed area below.

I had gone several miles and had not seen a sheep since my field-glasses had revealed those on the mountain behind camp. . . .

July 29—Early in the morning I climbed a little knoll near-by. . . . Two miles to the north-west, near the top of the smoother portion of a high spur which projected out from the slope, I saw twelve sheep, and more careful inspection revealed their spiral horns. Rams found so quickly! Hastening a mile down the creek to a point where a good view of the spur could be obtained, I seated myself to make a study of the situation. The spur, a high butte with two cone-shaped peaks rearing up from its grassy surface, was connected with the mountain by a knife-blade ridge rising almost vertically to a group of crags a few feet below the dominating peak—the highest in the vicinity.

Three of the rams were feeding near a fourth, which was lying down in front of the outside peak; three others were lying on the saddle between the peaks, two of them facing in opposite directions; five more feeding near them on the face of the spur, and one was lying down half-way up on the inside peak. There was no method of approach except in plain sight of the rams, and I waited for two or three hours in the hope that they would move to a position favorable for a stalk. Among them I noticed only three rams with large horns. They passed the time indifferently, feeding and resting, and though moving lazily, each kept constantly looking about—never neglecting the habit of alert watchfulness. No sentinel was posted at any time.

While I was waiting, a mile to the right along the slope appeared two rams travelling rapidly, now walking, now running, in the direction of the band. By observing their horns, I judged one to be five years old, the other, two or three. At first I thought they were detached members of the band hurrying back to join it. But reaching the spur they caught sight of the sheep above, approached cautiously to within a hundred yards and stopped, as all the rams jumped up and watched them. Several times they circled about the band without approaching nearer, while the rams in the band appeared to assume a threatening attitude. Finally they passed the band without attempting to enter it, and disappeared around the slope.

Repeated observations of the habits of sheep in later years gives me a clue to the actions of these two rams. They were members of another band of rams living in another part of the ranges, and having been separated by fright, or for some other reason, were probably trying to regain their own band, composed of members with which they had been born and reared. Bands of sheep have a strong tendency to exclude foreign members, and it is only after a single sheep or two have hovered about another band for days, sometimes even for weeks, that its members relax and admit the outsiders on terms of intimacy. . . .

At two in the afternoon, all the sheep slowly fed over the top of the spur and were lost to sight. At once I began to follow the plan worked out while waiting, and started to make the ascent of a high promontory protruding from a mountain opposite the spur and separated from it by a deep cañon, the head of which I might be able to climb around, and, if possible, cross the face of the spur and stalk the sheep if they should be feeding on the other side. In an hour I had ascended far enough to see that the ground at the head of the cañon was too precipitous to traverse. The only alternative was to find a way to the bottom of the cañon and ascend the slope of the spur to the two peaks. This involved great risk of frightening the sheep, for if they should be feeding on the other side near the top, now and then, according to their habits, one or another would probably come back to inspect the opposite side, in which case I would surely be observed. But knowing that the next day they might be far away, I decided to take the chance, and after much difficulty reached the bottom of the cañon and climbed up a notch in the opposite wall to some willows through which, in half an hour, I had fought my way, reaching a smooth, grassy slope that led steeply upward between the peaks. No sheep had re-appeared above, so I began to ascend slowly and cautiously, knowing that at any moment a ram might suddenly appear on the summit and see me if I was moving.

Step by step I advanced, keeping as low as convenient, stopping every few feet and lying flat, always intently watching the crest above. My caution was increased as I came within rifle-shot of the top, and with rifle cocked, ready to fire at any ram that might appear, I finally reached a point within a few feet of the crest. There I rested a few moments to get my breath and steady my nerves. Then, creeping forward over the top, I slowly raised my head and looked over. Not a ram was visible. A succession of rocky walls, broken and rugged, jutting out in a curve from the spur, obstructed the view toward the mountain. Retiring from the sky-line, I went a short distance around the outside cone and, creeping forward, again looked over. I could then see the whole area below, but no rams were there. The slope fell to a creek, on the opposite side of which sheer cliffs rose up to the rocky débris covering the side of the mountain. I knew that the rams had ascended and were somewhere near the higher crest above.

But one resource was left, and that was to climb the rim of the spur to the highest peak of the mountain. From there it would not be difficult to clamber along the crest and possibly find the rams in a place favorable for stalking.

That ascent of fifteen hundred feet I shall never forget. The connecting roof-ridge was so narrow that for most of the distance it was not more than a foot or two wide. The view in the direction of the sheep was cut off by projecting crags. On either side sheer precipices or confused vertical masses of sculptured rock fell several hundred feet to the inclined surface below. The knife-edge, however, had been carved by the elements—eroded just enough so that small, sharp projections of rock, like an irregular series of teeth, protruded and provided a foothold. Slinging my rifle over my back and holding on the sharp nodules of rock above I toiled upward on this rough ladder-like precipitous path. I had started at four, and it was six P.M. when I reached the base of the pyramidal peak which rose fifty feet above the crest-line. The altitude was seven thousand eight hundred feet—more than five thousand feet above camp.

There I rested for a few moments. Not a sound reached my ears except the tinkling of the rills trickling down from the snow. A stupendous mountain panorama surrounded me. When my breath was regained, and the excitement owing to the danger of the climb was subdued, I started to creep along the narrow rocky crest which, twenty feet farther on, was so abruptly broken that I could not see beyond. After going ten feet on my knees, I saw a pair of horns perfectly motionless, a hundred and fifty yards ahead and slightly below. Nothing more, but I knew that a ram was below them. Stretching on my stomach, foot by foot I crawled ten feet to the edge of the break, where I was thoroughly concealed by a crag rising three feet above the surface and falling perpendicularly to the crest below. Carefully moving my head to the side of the rock, I looked down. There were the twelve rams a hundred yards away, all lying down without any suspicion of the enemy who now had them at his mercy. All were facing in the same direction, looking down the slope up which they had ascended. Below, at the bottom of the valley, was the winding creek, gleaming through the dark green of the spruces. In front of them were piled precipice upon precipice. They were at the edge of a brink which behind them fell fifty feet to a desolate basin of shattered rock filled with boulders and surrounded with turreted cliffs and craggy buttresses.

Their mixed colors were those common to the sheep of the region, the dark ones predominating; their heads, with the exception of three, were white. Each maintained an alert watch both in front and along the crest opposite to me. They kept jerking their heads to fasten their piercing gaze in those directions only; no danger could come from behind without their hearing it; the peak was in my direction, where they evidently felt safe from approach. I was facing the sun and could not take a photograph. Only three of the rams had large horns, the rest varying in age from five to three years.

Lying on my stomach and resting my rifle along my arm on the side of the rock, I fired at the ram which appeared to have the largest horns. At the crack of the rifle all jumped up and for a moment stood in wild confusion. The bullet had apparently gone true, for the ram simply stiffened out without rising and died. But another of the rams with large horns was holding his head in the air, his lower jaw falling loosely and bleeding. He suddenly dashed over the precipice, followed by the third with large horns, and by two small rams. Somehow reaching the foot, they again came in sight and dashed across the broken rock under some cliffs by my right, where they were lost to sight. Not hearing any more sounds of their running and knowing that they were standing, I remained perfectly still. The rest continued to stand and look, jerking their heads in all directions except toward me. None had even suspected the direction of the shot.

I watched the cliff for about three minutes, until a ram with large horns suddenly appeared, running down the slope. When a hundred yards distant, he stopped, long enough to receive a bullet in his heart. Then I heard a clatter of hoofs on the cliff, and saw the ram with the broken jaw leap on the top and stand on the skyline looking in the direction of the last ram I had killed. As I shot, he fell over the wall of the cliff and caught in a rift near the foot, where he remained doubled up and almost suspended. The other three had descended to the band, which, having run for a few hundred yards, had scattered and stood looking, not even then having located the direction of the shots.

Sitting on the rock, I rested and smoked my pipe. Three hard-earned trophies were before me. Under such circumstances, among mountain-crests, when the pulse bounds and the whole being is exhilarated by the intensely vitalizing air, while the senses, stimulated by the vigorous exercise of a dangerous climb and the sustained excitement of the stalk, are attuned to the highest pitch of appreciation of the Alpine panorama, there is no state of exaltation more sublime than that immediately following the climax of a day's successful hunt for the noble mountain ram.

The Stone or Black Sheep
Ovis dalli stonei

THE STONE OR BLACK SHEEP is a handsome fellow. His grayish-blue-black coat is rich and lustrous and is strikingly accentuated by his vividly white nose, broad white rump-patch, and neat, white trim running down the back of each leg. He is a slightly larger sheep than his all-white cousin, the Dall, but something less in height and weight than his not too distant neighbor, the Canadian Bighorn. Dufresne gives him a shoulder height of around 39 to 40 inches and a weight for a big ram of from 210 to 220 pounds, which is about the maximum. His horns are gracefully shaped, with medium corrugations, and are generally darker in color than those of the White sheep.

He ranges the grassy foothills and valleys of the rugged but comparatively low mountainous country of the southern Yukon and adjoining northern British Columbia. As the Dall-group map (Map 5) shows, his range comes very close to, if not in actual contact with, that of the White sheep in the southwestern Yukon.

Here the intrusion of a degree of white in his pelage is suggestive of intergradation, and here likewise the near-by White sheep sometimes show an intrusion of black hair. It is for this reason that an intermediate subspecies was described by Hornaday as *Ovis dalli fannini*. However, this subspecies has been dropped on the premise that, being so variable, it is but a color variation and not a constant factor warranting a separate race denomination. Ian McTaggart Cowan places this area of intergradation as the northern Cassiar and Pelly Mountains in the south-central Yukon.

The Stone sheep do not seem to have the same tendency to extremely flaring or nipped-in horns as the White sheep. However, heads with these variations are not infrequently to be found among them.

The opposite photograph of the complete mount of a Stone sheep shows a seven-year-old ram in short, early-fall pelage with the typical pattern of the white areas.

The Stone or Black sheep, in a mount by the author

With age the face of a Stone sheep begins to whitten, the white sometimes continuing down the neck and over the shoulders, which may become nearly all white in very old rams. However, this does not mean that when a Stone sheep carries a great deal of body white, it is necessarily a creeping process from the head or other white areas, for individuals may carry some whitish areas at birth, which is an indication of intergradation with the white Dall. Only

169

The world's record Stone sheep is this twelve-year-old ram taken by
L. S. Chadwick, in 1951, on the Muskwa River, British Columbia. The
measurements are: H.L. 51⅛"; H.B.C. 14¾"; H.T. 31". The mount
is by the author.

within the limited area between the Cassiar and Pelly Mountains
in the south-central Yukon, where the White and Black sheep have
met and intergraded, do we find evidence of such color intrusion.
And it is interesting to note that the farther removed the Black

sheep are from the point of contact with their white cousins, the less this intrusion of white shows. This would seem to indicate that intergradation is of comparatively recent date; otherwise the "white" would have, over a long period of time, filtered throughout the whole Black race, and likewise the "black" would have intruded into that of the White race.

Stone or White sheep showing signs of any color variation (black or white) are now considered to be but varieties of the Stone sheep.

"Record on a Meat Hunt"

ONE CAN NEVER TELL what might happen on a hunt, and so it was with L. S. Chadwick when he left his first sheep camp for a short sojourn to pick up some meat for the pot. Returning home, he wrote up what happened to him on that memorable day.

This story, written under the above title and over his name, "as told to Walter E. Burton," appeared in *Outdoor Life Magazine* (June, 1937), and the world's record Stone sheep head, which he brought back to camp, still stands as the record to this day. I here quote Mr. Chadwick from *Outdoor Life Magazine*:

Going out after food, and coming back with a sheep whose horns measure fifty-two and an eighth inches along the outside curve may be something new in hunting, but that's the way I bagged the head that apparently sets a new world's record for size.

The hunt really began eighteen days before I shot the ram. I had decided to look for sheep in a wild section of the Rocky Mountains in British Columbia because, on a previous trip, one of my guides had told me that there were some excellent specimens in a small region apparently never hunted by a white man.

My party consisted of myself and three guides, Roy Hargreaves, of Mount Robson, Walter "Curly" Cochrane, of Rolla, and Frank Golata, of Dawson Creek. Cochrane had operated a trap-line near the heaquarters of the Muskwa River five years before, and had seen many fine heads. All of these men are good guides, excellent hunters and trappers, and experienced outfitters. It was due entirely to their abilities that I located, and got, the record head.

We went into the sheep country from Pousse Coupé, a place I selected because it had a good hotel where I could stay while getting my outfit adjusted for the trail. From there, we went to Dawson Creek, seven miles farther up, and continued by automobile for eighty-five or ninety miles. We crossed the Peace River at Taylor Flats, and followed the river most of the time, going by way of Fort Saint John, to Bear Flat. There we picked up our pack train, and struck out into rough country. Going was often slow because, after leaving the regular beaten trails, we had to blaze our own. Some days we made only six or eight miles. We pitched sixteen camps in eighteen days, having twice to remain an extra day in camp because of heavy rains. We left Bear Flats August 9, and worked our way northwest, up Halfway River, over the two Nelson Summits, past Redfern Lake, and then turned north. We fought mosquitoes and gnats all the way.

When we pitched camp on August 27, Curly, who at the time was acting as cook, demanded that some of us go out and get a supply of fresh meat. "We've been living on bacon long enough," he complained. And the rest of us agreed. When you eat bacon day after day for more than two weeks, you develop a craving for something fresher.

We had arrived at about 2:30 in the afternoon, so there was plenty of daylight left. Roy, Frank, and I took the glasses and rifles, and started out to scout. We decided that, although we were looking primarily for fresh meat, we would not shoot any sheep unless they had fairly good horns. Thus the scouting expedition had the double goal of food and trophies, but we never suspected that it would turn out the way it did.

Soon after leaving camp, we split up. Roy climbed to the highest point on a near-by mountain that faced our camp, and set the 20× telescope on its tripod. Through the 'scope, he searched the neighboring ranges for sheep. He saw about ten or a dozen rams, but none that seemed to have horns larger than thirty-five or thirty-six inches. Then, six or seven miles away, he located three sheep on the sky line of a high mountain range. "One of them looks as if it might be worth going after," he declared. Pursuit, though, was impossible in what remained of that day.

Early next morning, however, we started after the three rams, hoping that they had not strayed very far from the place where Roy had spotted them. We were optimistic, so we took horses to bring back the meat. About 1 o'clock, we stopped to eat lunch up under a cliff, out of the wind. Not far away there was a high saddle of ground, near the top of the range. Lunch over, we climbed to the saddle, and surveyed the country with our glasses. We saw three sheep on top of a neighboring mountain, maybe a mile and a half away. One of the rams seemed to be carrying a wonderful pair of horns. We promptly decided to attempt a stalk.

The sheep apparently saw us. So Roy and I left the horses with Frank, who kept them out in the open, where the sheep could watch them, and started after our game. We went down to the valley between the two ranges, along the edge of a glacier that partly filled a steep ravine, then crossed the valley, and scaled the other side. Of course, when we got to our goal, the sheep were gone, but we soon sighted them in the next valley.

From this point, the biggest ram didn't look so promising. Roy and I debated whether to keep after him, or try to locate something better. We decided finally to keep on, now that we had gone this far, and get some pictures of him at least. Besides, we needed meat.

... I also like to shoot wild game with a motion-picture camera, particularly game I am going to try to bag with a rifle. So we crept within 200 yards or so of the sheep, and I exposed come color film on him.

* * *

Finally, I decided to try a shot. I fired from a sitting position, and, as he was directly below me, and almost straight down, I aimed a bit low. I was using a telescope sight for the first time on game of any size. The bullet struck the ram low in the body without hitting any bones, and the ram left in a hurry. Roy and I took after him. All the sheep ran swiftly down the valley for a short distance, and then started to climb our side of the mountain. The wounded one soon began to lag behind, and, while he was running down the valley I took four more shots at him before he disappeared. One of the bullets struck him lightly in the hip. I shouted to Roy, who was able to make much faster time than I, to give him a finishing shot. I felt that the sheep was so badly wounded that he eventually would die, perhaps suffering for hours or days before he did.

Roy was fast outdistancing me in the chase. When a man gets to be sixty-two, he has to move a little more leisurely than when he was young. I probably won't do much more hunting in a country where I have to climb mountain ranges 10,000 feet high.

The wounded ram was unable to keep up with the others on the upward climb, allowing Roy to get near enough to get in the finishing shot. The bullet passed through the sheep's body, back of the shoulder and above my first one. The animal dropped down into a deep ravine. When we got to him, he was dead.

Even then we were not too enthusiastic about our prize, a Stone ram (*Ovis stonei*). His body was small, at least for such a pair of horns. The big surprise came when we put the tape on him. The left horn measured fifty-two and one eighth inches along the outside curve, and thirty-one and a quarter between the tips. The circumference of the horns at the bases was a little more than fifteen inches. We were so excited that we failed to notice then that a small portion of the point, perhaps two and a half inches, was broken from the right-hand horn. Except for this, I am sure the right-hand horn would have been at least a half inch longer than the left, as it was larger at the base and throughout its length.

I remembered that the largest previous bighorn head on record had horns measuring about forty-nine and a half inches on the outside curve, so I obviously had the biggest wild-sheep head ever taken. Later checking showed that the finest sheep head of any species listed in "Records of North American Big Game" is that of the bighorn credited to James Simpson, who shot it in British Columbia in 1920. The horns had an outside curve of forty-nine and a half inches and a spread of twenty-three and seven eighths inches. The largest Stone-sheep head, a trophy taken by C. R. Fahr on the Peace River in 1930, had a curve of forty-four and three quarters inches.

By the time Roy and I reached the dead sheep, Frank had become tired of waiting, and had started with the horses to follow us. Just as we were planning to go back and look for him, he appeared in the valley, scarcely 400 yards below. As he was able to lead the horses within 100 yards, we did not have to carry our meat very far.

We estimated, from rings on our ram's horns, that he was about fourteen years old. He had excellent teeth, and otherwise was in good condition. All three men with me checked the measurements.

To my knowledge, Stone sheep are found only north of the

Peace River. There are no sheep of the common bighorn variety in that region. Stone sheep are smaller in body than regular bighorns, and have very different markings. Whereas the bighorn has a white "doughnut" on its rump, the Stone sheep has a white patch that extends all the way down to the ankles, like a pair of white pants. Its bluish-gray coat hasn't so much brown as the bighorn. The backs of the legs are white, the under body white or gray, and the fronts of the legs brown. Some specimens have white faces and necks.

*   *   *

Curly Cochrane told me there seemed to be only about one fifth as many sheep in the territory near the headwaters of the Muskwa River as there had been five years before. Wolves, he said, were responsible. If something isn't done to clean out the wolves, it won't be many years until the sheep are extinct in that region. The wolves get them when snow drives them down into the valleys.

At a sulphur spring near where we camped, I shot a big male wolf, the leader of a pack of five. In every direction from that spring I found sheep horns, some of them very good. Such slaughter cannot help but thin out the sheep.

Chances of getting heads bigger than the one I took probably are none too good, for big heads are becoming scarce wherever hunters are active, because of the practice of shooting rams with horns no larger than thirty-five or thirty-six inches around the curves. Too many hunters shoot rams with small horns, and then wonder why no big trophies are left. The only reason I was able to get the big fellow in the Muskwa River country was that no other hunters had been through there to get him when he was smaller. He happened, too, to be lucky enough to escape the wolves. As we did not cover this entire section, on account of heavy snow, there is a chance that some lucky hunter will some time find this old boy's daddy with a still larger head.

Most persons ask me what kind of rifle I use. My favorite for all types of big game hunting is a .404 Magnum, made by the late

Frank Huffman, of Cleveland. It shoots a 300-grain bullet at a muzzle velocity of 2,709 feet a second, and has about twice the power of a Springfield. With a heavier load, it is suitable for African game. There is no game in North America that it cannot kill with a 300-grain bullet. The gun weighs about ten pounds.

My guide always carries my Model 54 .30/06 Winchester. In case anything happens to the big gun, the Winchester will then be on hand, ready for business.

I realize the Magnum is a bit heavy for Rocky Mountain sheep, but I like its range, power, and accuracy. It has a remarkably flat trajectory. As for the range, a little experience I had with the second sheep I shot on my trip may illustrate that. I got within about 350 yards of him, and succeeded in taking some motion pictures through a telephoto lens. Roy suggested that, if I wanted that ram, I had better use the gun instead of the camera, because the sheep was moving away.

So I started shooting. I fired six shots, using iron sights, but missed because the animal was far away and moving fast. Then I decided to try one shot with the 'scope sight, as I could no longer see him with the naked eye. We judged the animal to be a good half mile away, but the bullet struck him in the hip, and did plenty of damage. It was pure luck that I hit him, but the shot does illustrate the power of the Magnum 300-grain bullet at such ranges. In the Stone-sheep country, it is difficult to get closer than 200 yards to one of the animals, because they have been made shy by constant attack from wolves. So a gun with considerable hitting power and flat trajectory is necessary.

This second sheep, by the way, had horns measuring forty-two inches around the curves, and thirty inches between the tips. It really was a much more beautiful specimen than the record one, and its horns were superior in color and general appearance.

I found plenty of other game north of Peace River, but used my movie camera more than my guns. In a basin on the south fork of the Muskwa River, we came upon a grizzly bear. I took movies of him, while he was stripping leaves from weeds and bushes, and eating them. Then I decided to try the rifle. I left the camera standing, and moved about seventy-five feet upstream, to be closer for the shot.

The first bullet struck the bear, and he came plunging down the little valley toward me. One of the guides decided to try his luck as a cameraman, so he aimed the moving-picture camera, and pressed the release. As the bear got fairly close to us, the camera developed a decided tendency to wobble. On the film, which we saw later, the image of the bear jumps wildly all over the scene. And the closer the bear gets to the guide, the more it jumps.

I finished the bear with a shot at close range, but the guide didn't know until afterwards that my gun had jammed because the follower plate had flipped over as I was loading by hand, and that the bolt of the rifle, which the other guide was getting ready to fire, had slipped out of the gun. If he had known, I don't suppose the bear would have stayed in the picture at all. Fortunately, I had shot grizzly before, and was able to keep my feet on the ground while I got my rifle loaded.

I had planned to go about 100 miles farther north, but snow prevented. However, I felt more than satisfied with the results of the trip. A number of other hunting expeditions into Alaska, Alberta, British Columbia, and Ontario had taught me that it is almost a rule that the prize trophy is taken on the very last day. The sensible thing to do, now that I had my trophy, was to quit, even if I had bagged it the first day with the first shot. The next time I hunt, it might not be a bad idea to go looking for meat instead of trophies.[1]

[1] In Appendix VII there is an interesting comparison of Chadwick's record head and the world's best Asiatic Bighorn head.

THE AMERICAN BIGHORNS

Ovis canadensis

Courtesy of The American Museum of Natural History

Canadian Bighorns, from a group in The American Museum of Natural History. The setting is in the Alberta Canadian Rockies between Jasper and Banff. The group was designed and supervised by the author.

The horns on the sheep to the right are Number Three in the world's record list. Immediately behind the center and left-hand sheep are the gentle, grassy grazing grounds so much preferred by the Bighorns.

SOME TWO HUNDRED MILES southeast of the Dall sheep ranges, in the mountainous country dividing Alberta and British Columbia, we come to the most northerly limit of the American Bighorns. We are indebted to Ernest Thompson Seton's book *Lives of Game*

Animals for some very interesting historical data regarding them which I summarize as follows:

"The first sighting of an American wild sheep was recorded from California by Coronado in 1540, but it was not until 1697 that a fuller description came from a Mission Father named Francis Maria Piccolo. And not until 1800 was it known that they existed elsewhere. When Duncan McGillivray and David Thompson, while exploring the waters of the Bow River near Banff, came upon a band of sheep and recognized them as something new, they saved a complete specimen.

"This new animal was first described by Dr. George Shaw in 1804 and named *Ovis canadensis*. Shortly thereafter others also described it, one naming it *O. carvina* and another *O. montana*, names which lasted for over a hundred years. But as three different names for the same sheep only confused the literature, Dr. Osgood of the Chicago Museum, in 1914, through due process and channels, returned to it its original name *O. canadensis*, by which it is now known."

From Alberta and British Columbia, we find the Bighorns closely following the mountains southward into the United States: through Montana, Idaho, Utah, Wyoming, Colorado, and into the northern section of New Mexico. From here on the "Desert" sheep take over, to continue into northern Mexico and down the peninsula of Lower California where the eastern end of the wild sheep's Great Arc terminates.

The Bighorn group consists of the "type" species, *Ovis canadensis canadensis*, and eight subspecies.[1] Although not as big in body and horns as the big eight in the Argali family, the American Bighorn, especially the more northern *canadensis* of Canada (often called the Canadian Bighorn), is truly a magnificent animal. His three hundred or more pounds of body weight and his heavy, massive horns place him a very close second to the Argali as a trophy.

Packed with power, self-assurance, and dignity, his sturdy body looks even larger than it really is by virtue of the shorter-boned

[1] For the classification listing of the American Bighorn group, see Appendix VI.

After Seton (1929) and Cowan (1940)

Map 6. Distribution Map of the American Bighorns. 1, *Ovis canadensis canadensis*; 2, *Ovis canadensis auduboni*; 3, *Ovis canadensis californiana*; 4, *Ovis canadensis sierra*; 5, *Ovis canadensis nelsoni*; 6, *Ovis canadensis mexicana*; 7, *Ovis canadensis texiana*; 8, *Ovis canadensis gaillardi*; 9, *Ovis canadensis cremnobates*; 10, *Ovis canadensis weemsi*.

legs, so well adapted to swift and strenuous climbing. His very rich, almost purple-brown coat, vivid white muzzle, and white rump-patch together with the white trim outlining the back of all four legs make him a very impressive sheep indeed—the best that America has to offer.

The Rocky Mountain Bighorn
Ovis canadensis canadensis

THE TEN-AND-ONE-HALF-YEAR-OLD RAM pictured above is Number Ten in the world's record list. It is a very massive head, which not only carries its heavy horn circumferences through to its tips but carries the curl of each horn through to something more than a complete circle. This is the type of head which sheep hunters and guides seem to prefer.

The data on this head read: taken by J. Benson Marvin, Western Alberta, 1924; H.L. 47"; H.B.C. 16"; H.T. 23".

It is interesting to note that this head's horn-circle diameter, which is exceptionally small, brings the lower, outer edge of the horns on a line with the lower jaw. In general aspect and conformation these horns are therefore not unlike those of the Tibetan Argali.

As far back as 1907, in *Campfires in the Canadian Rockies*, William T. Hornaday made an interesting observation regarding the particular locality where one would have the best chance of obtaining a really fine Bighorn: ". . . the biggest horns [of the Rocky Mountain Bighorns] have all come from southeastern British Columbia and adjoining southwestern Alberta, within a two-hundred-mile radius of Banff [Alberta]." This is still true, for several of the top world's record Bighorns have been taken within this area since 1920.

Hornaday, hunting in the Kootenay country in the southeast

A very good American Bighorn's head, mounted by the author

corner of British Columbia, took actual measurements and weights that are well worth repeating, for such complete and accurate field data are very rare. They are as follows: No. 1, thirteen-year-old ram: S.H. 41″; weight by scale 314 lbs.; skull and horns only (dried) 38 lbs. No. 2, ten-year-old ram: S.H. 40″; weight by scale 285 lbs.; skull and horns only (dried) 26 lbs.

Audubon gives the weight of a sheep which he obtained (presumably *Ovis canadensis auduboni*) at a total of 344 pounds, with the skull and horns at 44½ pounds. It is possible that this skull and horns were still "green" and not dried. My own Poli skull and horns weighed (dry) but 25 pounds. It is generally conceded that a big *canadensis* ram will measure 42 inches at the shoulder and weigh from 300 to 325 pounds. Of six *Ovis canadensis canadensis* skulls measured, the average over-all length was a little over 12⅝ inches, the longest being 13½inches. The maximum horn length recorded is 49 inches and the maximum base circumference 18 inches, but both these measurements are very rarely attained.

There is little tendency toward flare or divergence in the horn growth of the Rocky Mountain Bighorn. But in Alberta one notes a marked trend to a tighter curl, with the horns sometimes hugging the cheeks very closely. The Number Three world's record Bighorn, of 49-inch horn length (pictured above), is from this locality and has horns which curl to make more than a complete circle. Ned Frost told me that he knew of three different groups or bands of Wyoming Bighorns within a radius of one hundred miles of Cody, with each group carrying different types of horns: those with flaring or diverging horns, those with parallel-beamed horns, and those with the converging or nipped-in horns.

When a hunter had a particular preference for one of these types, Ned would take him to the band in which they predominated; and it is not strange that this should be possible, for apparently they were bands which had long been isolated and into which no new blood had been carried. Hence, through time they perpetuated their predominant type of horn growth.

My First Sheep Hunt

As previously mentioned, my very first sheep hunt was for the Rocky Mountain Bighorn in Wyoming, in the fall of 1907. My outfit was made up of Ned Frost as guide, my good friend Will Richards (a hunter in his own name) as cook, and three saddle- and eight pack-horses. I helped with the wrangling of the horses and the many chores about camp, which was not only much fun but good exercise.

In the golden month of September with clear blue skies and flamboyant autumnal foliage we often slept under the stars, lulled to sleep by the plaintive tinkle of the horse-bells and at times by the distant bark of a lone coyote. After spending two weeks in Yellowstone Park, where I photographed and studied its wild game, we headed southward toward the hunting country.

The author's pack train in the sheep mountains of northwestern Wyoming. Sheep graze and rest on the open, grassy meadows, but when alarmed they take to the rocky slopes for refuge.

It had been lovely in the Park and I regretted leaving its beauty and wonders: the Yellowstone Falls with its multicolored canyons, the fantastic hot springs and vividly colored mineral-springs, Old Faithful geyser, and the Hell Hole Basin with its many steam jets. But we had to be on our way to our hunting grounds.

I recall passing Old Faithful Inn about noon one day. Our pack train was trudging along, hot and covered with much road-dust, when a group of tourists hurried off the veranda of the Inn and hailed us to stop for a picture. After many pictures were taken the spokesman of the group waved us on with thanks, and as Ned passed him, he gave Ned a cigar. Then when Will came along in the middle of the line, he gave him a cigar. When I, now serving at the end of the line as horse-wrangler, approached, I saw him feeling for another cigar. When he could find none, he put his hand in his pocket and pulled out a quarter, and looking at me, covered

186

with dust and face unshaven, said: "Here, here's a quarter, buy yourself a drink." I accepted it—not knowing whether to be flattered as a cowboy or insulted as a drunk!

Leaving the Park by its southern entrance, we went southward to Jackson Hole and there turned eastward up the Buffalo Fork River, heading for the sheep grounds that lay another few days' trek to the east. On the Buffalo Fork, I hunted the wapiti and mule deer. And while I got my first wapiti, I missed out on the deer. Although the wapiti was a young bull I had a wonderful hunt along the sidehills of the valley, which was wooded with lodgepole pines. A heavy snow was falling softly, and there was not the slightest breath of air stirring. Fresh tracks in the snow warned me to be alert but I could see or hear nothing. Suddenly there was a sharp whistle—I knew that it was an elk which somehow had got my scent. He was somewhere above me. Then I heard the slight cracking of dead branches and the muffled thud of running feet—he was coming my way. I froze and waited. Then I saw him coming downhill at a fast trot, heading straight in my direction. Because I was motionless he did not detect me, and I waited until I feared that he would run me down. As I pulled up my rifle he put on the brakes, threw up his head in great surprise, and skidded to a stop only a few yards in front of me. In that split second I placed a shot squarely in his chest, and he fell to the ground and never moved. It was all over in but a few seconds.

Although he was not a large bull, he was a fine, fully adult animal and afforded me much excellent study; and I saved his complete skin and head as a Museum specimen.

It was a long day's trek up the Buffalo Fork to our sheep grounds, where we camped in small hidden valleys at the upper edge of the timber line. There we found water and wood for our camp and grazing for our horses. The first few days were spent in reconnaissance with as little disturbance as possible to the sheep. We wanted to find out where they were and the best way of approaching them. The valleys between these higher grazing grounds of the sheep were invariably steep, deep, and very rough. If one wanted to go to the next sheep ground across the valley it could mean a long detour to lower ground where the valley could be crossed, and then another stiff climb to the sheep pastures. And this could spoil the better part of a day. Although the area was good sheep ground it had, because of its relatively easy access, been heavily hunted for several years, and the sheep, although rather plentiful, were wild and cautious.

Sheep were spotted, but seemed to be always on mountains other than the one we were on. And when we would go to those mountains we would invariably see sheep in places where we had hunted the day before and found none. Finally we decided to move camp and try another area.

Forgetting the hunting for a day, we packed up to move to new ground, keeping to the valleys and out of sight as much as possible, which was not always easy. There was one high pass which we could not avoid, but a good glassing before we ventured the risk assured us that there were no sheep in sight and little chance that there would be while we were passing over. We mounted our horses and Ned led the way, to get over and out of sight in the shortest possible time. All went well until we were about halfway across. When Will shouted, "Sheep!" it was like a bombshell. There above us to the right was a small bunch of sheep, hell bent for the edge of the canyon. Where they came from we had no idea—they just suddenly appeared in the center of a grassy slope running up from the pass. I grabbed my gun, slipped off my saddle, and let fly two quick shots just as they went over the edge of the canyon and vanished. I was too excited to know whether I had hit one or not. But it made little difference since they were all out of eye range and well on their way. Ned and Will had held their fire to give me the first shots, and now they were running at top speed to the point where the sheep went over. I tried to follow but my sea-level lungs were no match for these mountain men and I soon had to slow down.

When I got to the edge Will told me that there was blood and that Ned had followed it. The canyon wall of treacherous loose rock dropped almost straight down, and I could see no sign of either the sheep or Ned. On my calling down to hear of his whereabouts, a call came back, faint as a faraway echo. Moving down the steep wall to a projecting cornice of rock, I could see Ned and my sheep, hung up on a ledge barely large enough to hold them. I had my first sheep—not by good shooting (for I couldn't remember whether I had the sights on him or not), but by sheer dumb luck!

He was a good ram, three or four years old, with fair horns and a good-sized body.

It was very precarious work measuring and skinning on that narrow ledge, where a slight misstep could have precipitated one to certain death. But with Ned's and Will's able help, the complete skin and head were saved as another Museum specimen.

I was but a neophyte at hunting and mountain-climbing and had much to learn. But this was a start and an experience which so enthralled me that I gladly sacrificed much to make the many trips that followed. Nothing seemed more worth while than to get out into the open—as close to the primitive and unspoiled as possible, where one lives not with man but with nature and wildlife, where complete freedom of body and soul is attained.

The Black Hills Bighorn

Ovis canadensis auduboni

THIS AUDUBON SHEEP is the only subspecies of the American Bighorns that is not included in the group of Desert sheep. Although probably now extinct, it enjoyed a large range just south of the Canadian border, from the state of Washington (where the type specimen was taken near Mount Adams) eastward through Idaho, Montana, Wyoming, and the western part of both Dakotas and northwestern Nebraska as far as the Missouri River. This is a large range for a subspecies, and *Ovis canadensis auduboni* must have transgressed right across the range of *Ovis canadensis canadensis*, which inhabited much of this area. If so, the two must have interbred, making both races along this path rather indefinite of identification. *Auduboni* is described as a large sheep with large skull, the largest molar teeth of all the *canadensis* group, and horns longer and more slender than those of the Canadian Bighorn.

Ernest T. Seton, in *Lives of Game Animals*, reports Audubon as giving the "weight of his fine Ram at 344 lbs., of which the horns [and skull] weighed 44½ lbs." These are the heaviest on record for any of the Bighorn group, which would indicate that *Ovis canadensis auduboni* may have been the largest of them all. But what we do not know is whether the horn-and-skull weight was taken when the head was "green" or dried. This could make a difference of a few pounds. One skull-length measurement of a four-year-old ram is given as 12½ inches.

Glover M. Allen, in *Extinct and Vanishing Mammals of the Western Hemisphere*, gives the following information on this sheep:

"Very slightly different from *canadensis* [with] light-grayish-brown coat. Rump and under parts grayish-white.

"Range: Country west of Missouri [River] in North Dakota and eastern Montana and Wyoming, where it must have intergraded with the Bighorns [*Ovis canadensis canadensis*].

"Believed to have their last stand in the Black Hills, where they were exterminated about 1895."

If one hears at this late date of sheep having been seen in the area of the Badlands of North Dakota, they may well prove to be some other sheep which, I understand, have recently been transported from elsewhere to this area, to repopulate this traditional sheep habitat.

THE DESERT BIGHORNS

THE SO-CALLED DESERT SHEEP are all subspecies of the northern Bighorn, *Ovis canadensis canadensis*. It is but an arbitrary term used for the southern, more arid, open-country Bighorns, inhabiting the extreme western and southwestern parts of the United States and the adjoining northern parts of Mexico.

Generally their habitats are very dry desertlike areas, where less favorable conditions have dwindled the size of bodies and horns and lightened the pelage color. This is particularly true of the Nelson sheep, which are the palest of all. Although they are somewhat smaller than their more northern cousin, their horns are sometimes quite massive, giving the effect of being too large for their bodies. The horns carry a tighter curl, with slight divergence and slightly turned-out tips. The corrugations are usually small and invariably show considerable wear, perhaps from the sheep's habit of using them to smash the big cacti for water and sometimes for food. Although the horns sometimes seem disproportionately massive for the bodies, they are in over-all measurement somewhat smaller than those of the northern Bighorns; and with the sheep's short-haired pelage their very small necks look far too weak to carry these weighty horns and to back them up in fighting. Apparently their neck muscles do not swell during the rut, as do those of the deer family.

Desert sheep will, of course, vary in height and weight, but as a group they will run from 36 to 40 inches at the shoulders, the latter height being about the maximum. In weight a big ram would range from 180 to 200 pounds, with 225 pounds as the maximum— all of which measurements would make them about the size of the Alaska Dall sheep.

Although most of the Desert sheep range south of their parent Bighorn group, there is one (*Ovis canadensis californiana*) which extends its range as far north as southwestern British Columbia, probably because postglacial conditions were favorable enough to encourage it to do so.

With some of these Desert sheep we have a situation much like that of the overlapping Urials, with the same uncertainty as to just "who's who" among them. Several previously named subspecies have since been considered invalid and have either been reclassified with their near-by neighbor or dropped from the roster completely. Here again we are reminded that unless we can say exactly where a particular sheep was taken, there is some difficulty in telling just what sheep it may be.

The Lava-Bed or Rimrock Bighorn
Ovis canadensis californiana

WE FIND THESE SHEEP in the coastal mountains of southwestern British Columbia and follow them down the Cascade Range through Washington and Oregon into eastern California, where they terminate along the Nevada-California border. Although they are now believed to be extinct, it is possible that a few may still be found within the northern limits of their range.

Their twelve-inch skull length indicates that they are but slightly smaller than their near-by cousins, the Canadian Bighorns, which range some 150 miles to the east. It is probable that these two sheep were at one time in actual contact, which would account for their close similarity at this northern end of their range. The *californiana* pelage is said to be a somewhat lighter brown than that of the Alberta Bighorns, yet Ernest T. Seton, in *Lives of Game Animals*, describes their pelage as "much darker."

Their horns are less massive and more divergent than those of *Ovis canadensis canadensis* and somewhat darker in color. The type specimen is given as taken near Mount Adams, Yakima County, Washington. They formerly inhabited the lava beds of eastern Oregon, northeastern California, and northern Nevada. Yet Seton gives their type locality as "east slope of Mt. Baxter, Sierra Nevada, Calif."

The photographs above show a seven-year-old ram measuring: H.L. 31½"; H.B.C. 14"; H.T. 21".

Although the horns are said to be lighter and slightly more divergent than those of the Rocky Mountain Bighorn, the picture shows a divergence perhaps something more than the average head of this race. Seton gives measurements of a Lava-Bed sheep taken by John Muir near the Modac Lava Beds of Mount Shasta as: S.H. 42"; H.L. 33"; H.B.C. 16"; H.T. 29½"; Ear length 4¾".

This long ear length reflects its close relationship to the Desert sheep rather than to the shorter-eared Rocky Mountain Bighorn. And although its shoulder height is that of a Rocky Mountain Big-horn ram, its flaring horn measurement of 29½ inches is quite beyond that of any *canadensis* head I have ever heard of. Yet the horns of *californiana* are said to have a spread wider than most Bighorns'.

The Sierra Nevada Bighorn

Ovis canadensis sierra

Courtesy of Jim Wellman

A Sierra Nevada Bighorn, photographed in the Santa Rosa Mountains, Riverside County, California.

THIS SHEEP RANGES the lower southern end of the Cascades in the Sierra Nevada Mountains running along the California-Nevada border from Mono County south to Mount Whitney. The type specimen was described from the eastern slope of Mount Baxter, California.

It is said to be very similar to its more northern cousin *Ovis canadensis californiana* but somewhat paler and grayer in pelage color. The ears are noticeably large, and muzzle and rump-patch are conspicuously whitish.

Ian McTaggart Cowan ruled out this subspecies classification, synonymizing it with *Ovis canadensis californiana*.

Nelson's or Desert Bighorn
Ovis canadensis nelsoni

Courtesy of the Los Angeles Museum of Natural History

The Nelson Bighorn sheep group in the Los Angeles Museum of Natural History. The scene presents a view of the Nelson sheep's habitat in Death Valley, California. The shoulder height of the six-and-one-half-year-old ram shown in the upper left-hand corner is 34½". Horn measurements: H.L. 28½"; H.B.C. 13¼"; H.T. 21½".

THIS NELSON OR DESERT SHEEP covers a rather large expanse of land encompassing the mountain ranges of Death Valley and the Mojave Desert, including almost the whole lower third of California and southern Nevada.

It is a comparatively small sheep, 35 to 38 inches at the shoulders.

Courtesy of the Academy of Natural Sciences

The Number Two world's record *nelsoni* was taken about 1892 in the Grapevine Mountains, Inyo County, California. Measurements: H.L. 44″; H.B.C. 17″; H.T. 23⅞″.

Although with generally lighter and slightly flaring horns, they sometimes attain a 44-inch horn length and a 17-inch base, as illustrated in the picture above.

They are perhaps the one sheep that truly justifies the colloquial name of "Desert sheep," since their habitat for the most part is true desert country. For this reason they have dwindled somewhat in size and taken on the lighter shades of the usual sheep-brown, the better to match their surroundings. One characteristic marking is that noted by C. Hart Merriam, in *Bighorn Skull from the Plains of Western Dakota*: "Their small white rump-patch is divided lengthwise to the base of the tail with a dark line." Their weight is reported as around 250 pounds. The data on the head shown in the above photographs are: H.L. 34½″; H.B.C. 15″; H.T. 24″. Skull length is around 12 inches.

As would be expected in a Desert sheep, the horns of Nelson's sheep are a light-reddish-yellow in color with medium-sized corrugations. The pelage is a light-buff with a little deeper reddish-yellow tinge on the neck and shoulders and a more grayish tinge on the under parts. The muzzle is a lighter shade of the body-color. It is said to be the palest of all the Desert sheep. It will be noted that the ears are small, which perhaps gives it a closer relationship to the northern Bighorn than to the more southern Desert sheep.

Merriam gives the type specimen as taken in the "Grapevine Mountains, east of Inyo County, California." It is said to be the most plentiful of all the Desert sheep.

The Arizona or Mexican Bighorn

Courtesy of the Academy of Natural Sciences

The Mexican Bighorn group in the Academy of Natural Sciences, Philadelphia. The setting for this group was taken near Port Libertad, Sonora, Mexico.

Mexicana is an inhabitant of the greater part of western and southern Arizona and the adjoining northern provinces of Chihuahua and Sonora in Old Mexico.

Widely but thinly distributed, *mexicana* (with its two varieties, *gaillardi* and *texiana*) is the only Desert sheep existing east of the Colorado River, which serves as an effective barrier, dividing this race from all other Desert sheep living beyond its western shore.

It ranks among the larger of the Desert sheep, carrying heavy, massive horns reflecting a rather sudden taper. Its particular feature is its long, pointed ears (4⅜"), which are said to be twice the length of those of the Canadian Bighorn.

The type specimen was taken near Largo de Santa Maria, Sonora, Mexico.

Horn measurements of the six-year-old ram shown in the above pictures: H.L. 35″; H.B.C. 15⅝″; H.T. 21″.

The horns are a dark reddish-brown with small but well-defined corrugations. One skull measured approximately 11½ inches in over-all length.

In *Bighorn Skull from the Plains of Western Dakota*, C. Hart Merriam notes the color as follows: "Body color above and below, dark brown, darkest on throat, legs and tail; muzzle decidedly paler than rest of face; rump-patch broader and more squarely truncated anteriorly than *O. c. c.*, but much less on lower legs, the white spreading broadly over the posterior and inner aspects and on the inner sides ending abruptly just above the calcaneum [heel bone] joint. Whitish of chin broader and less sharply defined."

My own notes, taken from the habitat group pictured above, read: "Horns pale yellow superimposed with a reddish brown (probably soil and oxidized vegetable saps). Pelage warm mouse-gray; white muzzle; little suggestion of white on under parts. Mexican sheep grayish-red rather than grayish-tan like that of Nelson's sheep."

On this sheep we now have many recent and reliable data presented in John P. Russo's booklet *The Desert Bighorn Sheep in Arizona*, which is one of the best publications of its kind in sheep literature and could well serve as a prototype to be followed by other states or countries interested in conserving their wild sheep. Regarding weight, Russo says: ". . . of 7 adult rams weighed, the average was 190½ lbs. . . . their probable weight in the fall would average around 200 lbs. When dressed their total lost-weight was ⅓."

Courtesy of George W. Parker

A Sonora Bighorn (*Ovis canadensis mexicana*), taken near Port Libertad, Sonora, Mexico.

According to George W. Parker, of Arizona, "a big, fat Arizona ram might go to 225 lbs."

Russo gives the average shoulder height of seven *Ovis canadensis mexicana* rams measured (apparently the same rams previously mentioned) as 36¹⁄₁₀₀ inches, with the largest as 39½ inches.

Range: "Their range covers about ⅓ of the State."

Rainfall: "About 3½ inches per year."

Color: "July rams in light summer coat chocolate-brown to gray."

Food: "Saguaro or giant-cactus eaten primarily for water; other cacti eaten for food."

George Parker has also written me on this subject: "Desert Sheep do knock over and eat the barrel cactus. They also butt the giant saguaro cactus and eat away the pulp. I can show you big areas in western Sonora where most of the cactus has been eaten over a period of many years. They do not do this in lower Cali-

Courtesy of John P. Russo, Arizona Game and Fish Department

Typical habitat of the Arizona Bighorn (*Ovis canadensis mexicana*), Tanjas-Atlas Mountain, Yuma County, Arizona.

fornia though. Nor do they bother the giant cactus much in other parts of Sonora."

W. T. Hornaday in his excellent book *Campfires on Desert and Lava* gives both good reading and data on these sheep, which he hunted in 1908, in and around the Pinacate Mountains lying in the extreme northwestern corner of Sonora just south of the Mexican border. Particularly interesting are his remarks concerning weights and measurements. One ram which he weighed went to 192½ pounds, with the best horn-base circumference running to 17 inches. Three other rams measured 15 inches or better in base circumferences. One ram measured 37 inches at the shoulders. All of this data reflects a rather large Desert sheep.

"Hornaday Hunts the Lava-Bed Sheep"

HORNADAY'S NARRATIVE of his hunt for the Desert Bighorn (*Ovis canadensis mexicana*) in the Pinacate Mountain regions of northwestern Mexico is both informative and amusing.

This whole region is a vast lava-strewn desert with many uplifts and sunken craters, all of which give it the well-deserved name of the Lava Beds. Here, with a minimum of water and a thin sprinkling of prickly, vicious desert flora, the Desert Bighorn lives and even thrives. And except for Weems' Bighorn on the Peninsula of Lower California, it is the southernmost of the Desert sheep.

With Hornaday were John M. Phillips, of Pittsburgh, and a small group of local experts and guides well qualified to cope with such an unfriendly land. Going in from Tucson, the party traveled by wagon and horseback, making camp in the open wherever they stopped—but I shall let Hornaday tell his own story:

"The nineteenth of November was a day of many sensations . . . the leader, Mr. Phillips, and I unanimously decided that the day should be devoted to hunting sheep. . . . A three mile tramp across a very interesting lava plain brought us to an isolated extinct volcano which rose a little to the northward of our course. . . . It was very imposing, very rough and admirably adapted to the wants of sheep, but no sheep were there.

On a commanding ridge we sat down . . . to scan the cones (volcanic) with our glasses. . . . We entered the roughest, wildest and most awfully upheaved volcanic region that we saw on the trip. There was a bewildering maze of deep valleys, high ridges, mounds and mountains, all of them covered with the roughest lava to be found anywhere under the sun. Every square yard of it was horrible. There were dozens of ravines which no horse could cross, even under an empty saddle, with a rider on foot, to lead the way. The slightest fall in that stuff would cut a man's knees and hands most cruelly. . . .

But it was a glorious day. . . . Presently we reached what we were sure was an elevation of two-thousand feet and the bird's-eye view of the lava field and its surroundings became genuinely fascinating. It was all so weird and uncanny we could not keep our eyes from it for long at a time. As we ascended, the strip of sand-hills became narrower and the glassy waters of the Gulf of California seemed to come nearer.

We hunted carefully, but saw no sheep, nor signs of them. For hours we had been steadily working into the heart of the roughest lava mountains in sight and quite rough enough they were, too!

At last we began to fear that in coming into such a blasted place we had overdone the situation: for why should Mountain Sheep, that usually love luxury, choose to live in such a petrified hell as that? So we both said, "Let's go on yonder red peak, and if we don't find sheep by that time, we may as well look elsewhere."

We toiled painfully up the sides of a great ridge, and as we reached the summit we scanned the new prospect with a sheep-hunter's usual caution. I chanced to be in the lead. The farther side of the ridge dropped to a considerable valley, which ran down rather steeply for a quarter of a mile to our right, where it joined another valley that came down at right angles from somewhere higher up. As we paused behind a stunted mesquite, hunting just as carefully as if there were a hundred sheep within range, our eyes swept the lava valley in front of us, from its head to its lower end. And *then* I saw two somethings—as big as cattle—so it seemed. "Look yonder! Two sheep! Rams, both of them! Merciful powers! Look at that head of horns!"

That was the only time in my life that I ever said "head of horns" but that head seemed to be *all horns*! As the leader of the two rams walked slowly into the other valley and disappeared behind the nose of the opposite ridge, he held his head low, as if his horns were so heavy that he could scarcely carry them.

We crouched behind our bush until the sheep were out of sight; then we did things. We saw that we had to run down our ridge and up the next one—a good half-mile in all—to reach a point from which we might hope to see the rams again; and within rifle shot, with unblushing effrontery, I took off the party canteen, half filled with water, and without a word handed it to John. Without even a wink of protest he put it on, over his camera. Then, feeling that it was my bounden duty to kill one of those rams and thereby relieve the tension of the party, I set off down the ridge-side as hard as I could run, with Mr. Phillips close behind.

We went down that ridge without a tumble, and at full speed raced up the other. That was the only creditable performance, in that I did not fall down and break something. In what was really very quick time, we covered that half-mile and reached the top of the ridge below where we expected to find two old "bungers." It was right there that the mistake of Moses began.

I was out of breath, and entirely too confident. Feeling that we had a "cinch" on those sheep, and that they were just the same as skinned and hung up, my advance over the top was too rapid and incautious. For one thing, I feared that they might be already far beyond us. Hurriedly, I overlooked the visible portions of the valley of big lava chunks and scattered mesquite bushes, but saw not a sheep. Scanning everything in sight, and fully expecting to see the sheep before they saw me, I advanced over the top of the ridge. Mr. Phillips saw one of the sheep behind a mesquite bush, down at the bottom of the valley, looking up at us, and he tried hard to tell me; but I was so crazy to locate the animals that I did not hear a sound.

Opposite us, and beyond the sheep-infested valley, there rose a red volcanic peak to a height of some hundreds of feet. The side facing us was very steep indeed, and off a little way to the right it terminated in a sharp nose around which we could not see.

My first sight of a sheep was when one of the rams suddenly appeared across the ravine on the side of that peak, and in mad flight. It was a good two-hundred yards away, and the sight almost gave me a horrible chill. The animal was not the ram with the heavy horns—though his horns were plenty big enough "to satisfy the taste of the most fastidious"—and to my horror he went away from me, *diagonally*, and also *upward*!

Instantly I fired at him, and overshot. Mr. Phillips cried "Lower! You're overshooting!" Again, and the bullet cut up dust beyond him. Again! There was no dust raised by the ball, but he did not *show* that he was hit. My thoughts were all on one line, thus: "Quick! Quick, or he will get around that point and be lost forever! Hurry!" Just then there was a rush of a dark object coming tearing over the lava from the left and below, straight toward us. One glance showed that it was the other ram, coming like a steam-engine!

"*Here he comes,*" yelled John, fifty feet to my right, in a tone of stern command. "Shoot *him*! Shoot *him*!"

With my eyes fast fixed on my own fast-vanishing ram, I threw a cartridge into the magazine of my Savage, and as the big ram rushed by only forty *feet* away, my muscles obediently pointed my rifle toward the animal. *Without taking the slighest aim*—with both mind and eyes firmly fixed upon my own escaping ram—I pulled the trigger. I never touched a hair of that ram—and afterward could scarcely believe that I had fired in his direction. It was not *my* ram, in any event; and my whole thought had been that I had no *right* to shoot at him!

An instant later Mr. Phillips' big rifle roared out at the ram, full into its vitals, as it passed him only twenty yards to his right, and "biff"! went the horns of the ram into the side of a niche in an upright rock, twenty paces further on. With the crash of the impact the splendid animal fell stone dead. Then Mr. Phillips whirled to me and said, "Oh! I beg your pardon, Director! I didn't mean to do that! *Please forgive me!*" I could have shouted with laughter at the glorious absurdity of that speech. It was too funny for anything to enjoy a laugh at that time. My running ram was almost to the vanishing point, and going as well as ever.

For what I knew was my last shot, I steadied myself, took more deliberate and careful aim, and let go. No visible result; and the next instant the sheep turned the corner and disappeared.

The awful mess that I had made of a perfectly golden opportunity, and the horrible exhibition that I made of myself, almost made me sick. I think that was the worst thing that I ever did in hunting; and that is saying much. But I resolved to do my best toward looking further for that ram. So I said, humbly, "I am going to circle around the base of that peak and see if I can find that ram again."

"Your third shot hit him, all right," said Mr. Phillips, "and it was bully good shooting—at that ram bouncing diagonally up those stairs: Your last shot was at four hundred yards. I'll go up yonder and take his trail and see what I can do."

"Well, don't fall off that steep place, ram or no ram."

We separated, and in a miserable frame of mind I swung off lower down, to encircle the base of the peak. The lava was bad as the worst, and my progress was maddeningly slow. I had really no hope of ever again seeing that ram, unless I found him dead.

After an interval, I saw Mr. Phillips gingerly working his way along the dangerous face of that steep pitch, and at last he called softly, from quite highup, "There's blood here! You hit him!"

I pushed on over the lava, faster than before, and actually made my big circuit faster than my comrade was able to make his small one on that dangerous slope. I had swung around nearly a mile in order to reach a spot such as the ram would naturally choose to lie down in if he were badly wounded. I was about two hundred feet lower down than the vanishing point. At last I started to climb up to the heart of the place where the sheep might well be if he were wounded and had not got clear away—and then I was fairly electrified by seeing the ram's head suddenly appear above me, and look down at me. The next instant, however, he vanished.

I went up that lava pile at a run, and soon stood where the ram had been. He was nowhere in sight but a great patch of blood-spatters showed where he had stood for some minutes. Eagerly my eyes devoured every object in sight. The ram might have gone any one of three or four ways; but I felt that in the end I would get him. Then I heard a voice, as if from Heaven, calling out from away up on the peak,

"To the right! To the right!"

I whirled and crashed off that way at top speed, and ran straight toward the sheep. He was just climbing up the ragged side of a deep ravine of lava about seventy-five yards at the top. As he reached the top I was quite ready for him, and planted my one good shot.

He fell over like a bag of wheat, tumbled slowly down the wall of ragged lava, and half way down lodged fast, hanging head downward. The chase was done; but the less said about the manner of it, the better. I did, however, shout the news to John M., who stood on his red peak, swinging his Stetson sombrero, and yelled his congratulations.

[Hornaday's ram's head measured 17 inches around the base.]

The Texas Bighorn

Ovis canadensis texiana

Courtesy of the Texas Game and Fish Commission

ALTHOUGH *texiana* has for some time been considered a valid sub-species of *canadensis*, some scientists believe it to be no different from *mexicana*. However that may be, we can perhaps best think of it as a variety of *mexicana*.

The type specimen was taken in the Guadalupe Mountains of El Paso County, Texas. The specimen shown in the photograph above was taken from the Sierra Diablo Range, north of Van Horn, Culberson County, Texas, about the year 1935 or 1936. According to the Texas Game and Fish Commission's estimate: "there are [now] approximately a dozen or so bighorns remaining in this area. ... It may be finally concluded that the small population remaining in the Sierra Diablo region are the last of the Texas Bighorn."

The shoulder height, taken from this mounted specimen, measured 35⅛ inches, coming within an inch or so of Russo's average of 36.01 inches for his seven *mexicana*. The horns on the mount pictured above show a very typical *mexicana* head, i.e., massive horn base with a quick taper and basically parallel beams carrying slightly turned-out tips. These horns measure: H.L. 32½"; H.B.C. 15½"; H.T. 17½". A very creditable head.

As in *mexicana*, the ears are large and conspicuous. In color we may expect *texiana* to be very similar to their near-by relation— rather light, grayish-tan-brown with under parts very slightly paler, the white face and muzzle much subdued, with a tinge of the same body-color.

Gaillard's Bighorn
Ovis canadensis gaillardi

Ovis canadensis gaillardi is another Arizona Bighorn which, like *texiana*, was for some time carried as a separate subspecies, but also later put in *mexicana*.

The type specimen was taken in southwestern Arizona between the Tinajas Atlas Mountains and the Mexican border. It apparently also transgresses the border into Sonora, for many specimens have been taken there. The photographs above show such a specimen taken by Kermit Roosevelt in the Sonora Desert in 1912. Besides the large ears, another distinguishing feature of *gaillardi* is said to be the wide space between the horn bases at the top of the skull.

The horn corrugations are of medium size but show considerable wear. One skull length taken measured 11¾". Another specimen taken in Sonora carried horns measuring: H.L. 31"; H.B.C. 14½"; H.T. 20½". Its age was seven-and-one-half years.

Gaillardi, like *nelsoni*, is said to be one of the smaller Desert sheep, but with a dark, drab pelage and without the white muzzle. The under parts are a slightly lighter shade of the body-color.

Lacking measurements, we may presume the size to be something a little less than that of *texiana*, i.e., 35 to 36 inches at the shoulders.

A Desert Bighorn, probably an *Ovis canadensis gaillardi* (now *mexicana*) because of the wide spacing between the horns at the top of the head.

Sheldon's Bighorn
Ovis canadensis sheldoni

SHORTLY AFTER THE TURN OF THE CENTURY C. Hart Merriam described another Desert sheep, collected by Charles Sheldon in the El Rosario area of Sonora, near the Gulf of California. This rare and little-known sheep, about 30 inches at the shoulders, appeared to be a variety of *mexicana* but because of its small size and other features was named by Merriam as the subspecies *sheldoni*. Later, however, it was found to be none other than a *mexicana* which had presumably strayed from its parent group in the Gila Mountains to an isolated and unfavorable habitat, to become dwarfed though little changed otherwise. Accordingly it was returned to *mexicana*.

Lower California Bighorn
Ovis canadensis cremnobates

Ovis canadensis cremnobates is a rather large, pale sheep, perhaps the palest of all, with massive horns and large ears. The type specimen was taken near Matomi, San Pedro Mártir Mountains, in the extreme northern part of the peninsula of Lower California. Although the major part of its range involves about one-fifth of the peninsula's total length, it also extends northward, west of the Colorado River, to transgress the adjoining border of California for a relatively short distance. Here *cremnobates* all but contacts the southwesternmost point of the Nelson sheep range. The extent of *cremnobates'* range southward on the peninsula is not definitely known.

The above photographs show a fine set of horns of an eight-year-old ram measuring: H.L. 42″; H.B.C. 15¼″; H.T. 25¾″. Its body-color is a pale-grayish-brown-tan, having the white of muzzle, rump, and under parts considerably subdued with a tinge of the same body-color. The horns are medium light in color, rather definitely corrugated, and considerably worn. One skull measured 11½ inches in length.

Weems's Bighorn

Ovis canadensis weemsi

In his *Lives of Game Animals*, Ernest T. Seton tells us that after Coronado reported wild sheep in America, some Jesuit missionaries, in 1697, not only saw sheep but carefully recorded their geographical position. From their detailed records there seems to be little doubt but that these sheep were none other than the ancestors of the present-day *weemsi* of Lower California.

As late as 1900 little was known of this southernmost sheep of the Western Hemisphere except that there were native reports of the presence of sheep in that area. Few if any white men had hunted them. It was not until 1936, when F. Carrington Weems, of New York, organized an expedition to enter this remote region to investigate these reports, that we gained definite knowledge of their existence and character. With Weems was an able mammalogist, E. A. Goldman, of the Smithsonian Institute of Washington, D. C.

Their objective was a range of mountains called the Sierra de la Giganta running parallel to the southeastern coast line of the peninsula of Lower California. They found a large, dark, short-haired Bighorn, different enough to be described as another sub-species of *Ovis canadensis*, and it was named *Ovis canadensis weemsi*.

Goldman wrote of his findings in *A New Mountain Sheep from Lower California*: "Local (type), the Sierra de la Giganta [Mountains], a narrow range, extending for a distance of 60-70 miles, close along the [southeastern] coast of Lower California. Range strongly uptilted toward the east. The western slope is more gradual, but along the crest the east front breaks away precipitously in a great series of gorges, ridges, and minor peaks and crags with contours labyrinthine in complexity.

"The highest peak, the Cerro de la Giganta, at the extreme north end rises to 5500 feet but the altitude of the general crest varies from about 3500 to 4500 feet. Permanent water is scarce but annual rain fall—as attested by vegetation—is somewhat more copious than in the central desert section of the peninsula. Vegetation subtropical, wild-fig, tall fan palms, beargrass. In this setting below 20° lat. mountain sheep reach their farthest south in America. Habitat conditions appear very favorable. Mt. lion present.

"Type—from Cajon de Tecomeja, Sierra de la Giganta, about 30 miles south of Cerro de la Giganta—alt. 2000 feet. Distribution: Sierra de la Giganta and northward toward *O. c. cremnobates* of no. lower California in the Sierra de San Borjas in the central part of peninsula.

"General Characters: Large size—color dark for a desert subspecies, pelage short; female horns remarkably long. Closely allied to *O. c. cremnobates*—size similar, but pelage shorter—color usually darker, varying to very dark brown more or less distinctly mixed with black. Similar in size to *O. c. gaillardi* but usually darker color than *O. c. nelsoni, mexicana* of Chihuahua or *O. c. texiana*.

"Color type above and below a very dark brown mixed with blackish admixture on back—legs and tail—rump patch white, nearly divided by medium line of longer dark hairs; fore and hind legs with white areas down inner surface to hoofs. Muzzle whitish—ears brown gray.

"Skull same size as *cremnobates*—horns of rams smaller base cir. and less flare. Skull larger and heavier proportions than *nelsoni*, massive widely spreading horns of rams approach those of *cremnobates* (male head in Smithsonian Institute). Skull closely approaching that of *cremnobates* but horns of *weemsi* not so spreading and less in base circumference than *gaillardi*. Skull similar in general size to *gaillardi*."

Measurement data on three sheep obtained by Goldman were: adult male, S.H. 40″; adult female, S.H. 38″; young male, H.L. 31⅝″, H.B.C. 13¼″, H.T. 16½″.

This sheep appears to be one of the larger, if not the largest, of the Desert sheep group, perhaps as large as the Lava-Bed sheep (*Ovis canadensis californiana*), for its skull measurements are about the same, plus or minus 12 inches. Of five adult rams' skulls which I measured the average was 11⁹⁄₁₀ inches, with two going to 12½ inches and three ranging between 11 and 12 inches.

The measurements on the sheep head shown in the photographs above are: H.L.33¾″; H.B.C. 15½″; H.T. 20″. This specimen, now in the National Museum, Washington, D. C., was taken near "Calmilli" at the northern end of the *weemsi* range some years before the Weems-Goldman expedition. It is shown here because it is the largest, best-formed head among the limited number to be found in the National Museum's collection.

The *weemsi* horns are basically parallel-beamed, with little tendency toward convergence or divergence. They are very dark in color with medium-sized corrugations.

Although these sheep must have, at one time, been in contact with *cremnobates* to the north (from which they probably branched off), it is not known whether or not their ranges now meet.

* * *

With this last chapter we come to the eastern end of the Great Arc of the Wild Sheep, and with it to the end of our story.

There is much scientific work yet to be done on this subject; let us hope and pray that the wild sheep may resist complete annihilation at the hand of man long enough to make this possible. They are far too noble an animal to let pass from this earth.

And let us be thankful to those dedicated conservationists of America and other lands who have done so much to save the few which now survive. But this is not enough. We must now help these bands of sheep in their fight for survival, building up their numbers by better protecting them with more rigid game laws, and by protecting if not enlarging their pastures in all the lands of their domain throughout the Great Arc.

A Scoring System for Evaluating the Over-all Excellence of Sheep Horns

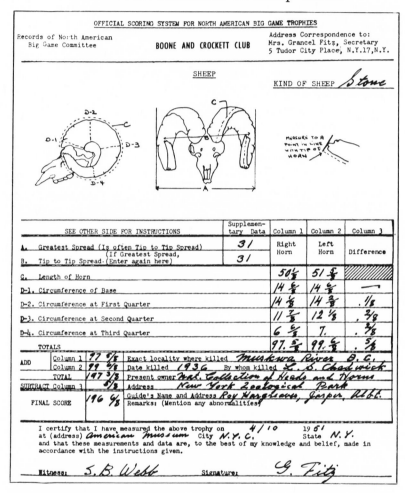

OFFICIAL SCORING SYSTEM FOR NORTH AMERICAN BIG GAME TROPHIES

Records of North American Big Game Committee

BOONE AND CROCKETT CLUB

Address Correspondence to:
Mrs. Grancel Fitz, Secretary
5 Tudor City Place, N.Y.17,N.Y.

SHEEP

KIND OF SHEEP *Stone*

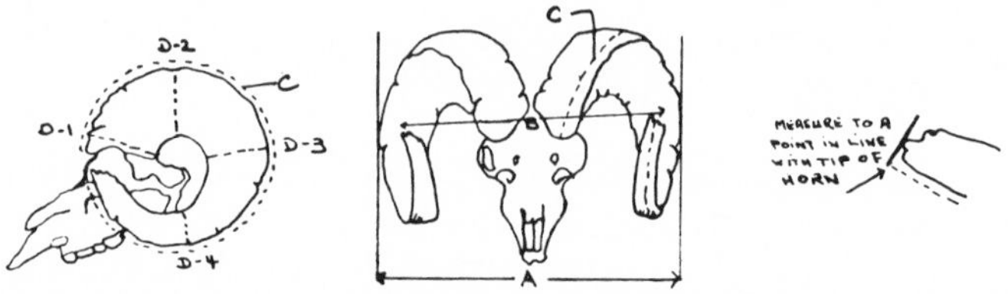

SEE OTHER SIDE FOR INSTRUCTIONS	Supplementary Data	Column 1	Column 2	Column 3
A. Greatest Spread (Is often Tip to Tip Spread)	31	Right Horn	Left Horn	Difference
B. Tip to Tip Spread (If Greatest Spread, Enter again here)	31			
C. Length of Horn		50 1/8	51 5/8	
D-1. Circumference of Base		14 6/8	14 6/8	—
D-2. Circumference at First Quarter		14 1/8	14 2/8	.1/8
D-3. Circumference at Second Quarter		11 7/8	12 1/8	.2/8
D-4. Circumference at Third Quarter		6 6/8	7.	.3/8
TOTALS		97. 5/8	99. 6/8	.5/8

ADD Column 1	97 5/8	Exact locality where killed *Muskwa River B.C.*
ADD Column 2	99 6/8	Date killed *1936* By whom killed *L. B. Chadwick*
TOTAL	197 3/8	Present owner *Nat. Collection of Heads and Horns*
SUBTRACT Column 3	5/8	Address *New York Zoological Park*
FINAL SCORE	196 6/8	Guide's Name and Address *Roy Hargreaves, Jasper, Alta.*
		Remarks: (Mention any abnormalities)

I certify that I have measured the above trophy on *4/10* 19*51*
at (address) *American Museum* City *N.Y.C.* State *N.Y.*
and that these measurements and data are, to the best of my knowledge and belief, made in accordance with the instructions given.

Witness: *S. B. Webb* Signature: *G. Fitz*

THIS SCORING SYSTEM with its format design (one of several for North American big game) was originated and first published by the author in July, 1935. Now used with some modifications by

INSTRUCTIONS

All measurements must be made with a flexible steel tape to the nearest one-eighth of an inch. To simplify addition, please enter fractional figures in **eighths.**

Official measurements cannot be taken for at least sixty days after the animal was killed. Please submit photographs.

Supplementary Data measurements indicate conformation of the trophy. Evaluation of conformation is a matter of personal preference.

A. Greatest Spread measured between perpendiculars at right angles to the center line of the skull.

B. Tip to Tip Spread measured from outer edge of tips of horns.

C. Length of Horn measured from lowest point in front on outer curve to a point in line with tip. DO NOT press tape into depressions.

D-1 Circumference of Base measured at right angles to axis of horn. DO NOT follow irregular edge of horn.

D-2-3-4. Divide measurement C of LONGER horn by four, mark BOTH horns at these quarters even though other horn is shorter, and measure circumferences at these marks.

ACKNOWLEDGEMENTS

The first complete system for scoring North American big game trophies was originated and copyrighted in 1935 by Dr. James L. Clark. The second was devised by Grancel Fitz in 1939 and published in NORTH AMERICAN BIG GAME. Recognizing the need for a single, standard system of accepted authority, the Boone and Crockett Club in 1949 requested an independent committee to develop the Official Scoring System for North American Big Game Trophies. The members of this committee were Dr. Harold E. Anthony, Milford Baker, Frederick K. Barbour, Dr. James L. Clark, Grancel Fitz and Samuel B. Webb, Chairman.

This Official System is basically a consolidation of the best points in the two previously existing systems. In the process, some new points have been developed, errors corrected, and needed simplification has been achieved.

Before publication, these charts were circulated to more than 250 qualified sportsmen, guides, authors, taxidermists, game officials, and scientists for constructive criticism and approval. The Boone and Crockett Club gratefully acknowledges the contribution of this group, and the work of the Committee.

Copyright 1950 by Boone and Crockett Club

2

(Written request for privilege of complete reproduction is suggested.)

the Boone and Crockett Club, it is a "point" system which considers and evaluates the several quality features of a sheep head and sums them up in a total score.

Classification of the Mouflons and Urials[1]

	RACE
Ovis musimon (species type)	Corsica
Ovis ophion ophion (species type)	Cyprus
Ovis ophion anatolica (subspecies)	Anatolia
Ovis ophion armeniana (subspecies)	Armenian
Ovis gmelini gmelini (species type)	Erzurum
Ovis gmelini urmiana (subspecies)	Urmian
Ovis gmelini isphahanica (subspecies)	Isfahan
Ovis orientalis (species type)	Elburz
Ovis laristan (species type)	Laristan
Ovis vignei arkal (subspecies)	Transcaspian
Ovis vignei bochariensis (subspecies)	Bukharan
Ovis vignei cycloceros (subspecies)	Afghan
Ovis vignei punjabiensis (subspecies)	Salt Range
Ovis vignei vignei (species type)	Ladak

Previously described subspecies recently reclassified:
Ovis vignei blanfordi now *Ovis vignei cycloceros*
Ovis vignei erskinei now *Ovis vignei orientalis*
Ovis vignei dolgopolovi now *Ovis vignei arkal*
Ovis vignei varenzovi now *Ovis vignei arkal*

Although there are several scientific classification listings of the Urials which may be used as a basis in reviewing these sheep, I am inclined to favor the above as perhaps the most realistic.

[1] After Harper, *Extinct and Vanishing Mammals of the Old World*.

Classification of the Ovis Ammon[1]

RACE

The smaller, most western Argalis:

Ovis ammon severtzovi	Kyzyl-Kum
Ovis ammon nigrimontana	Kara-Tau

The lighter, flaring-horn Argalis:

Ovis ammon poli	Russian Pamirs
Ovis ammon humei	Kashgarian
Ovis ammon karelini	Tien Shan, Kissyk-Kul
Ovis ammon littledalei	Tien Shan, Dzungarian

The massive, heavy-horned Argalis:

Ovis ammon sairensis	Sair Mountains
Ovis ammon collium	Semipalatinsk
Ovis ammon ammon (species type)	Altai or Siberian
Ovis ammon dalai-lamae	Altyn Tagh Mountains
Ovis ammon hodgsoni	Tibetan
Ovis ammon darwini	Mongolian

Previously described subspecies recently reclassified:

Ovis ammon heinsi now *Ovis ammon karelini*
Ovis ammon mongolica now *Ovis ammon darwini*
Ovis ammon jubata now *Ovis ammon darwini*
Ovis ammon comosa now *Ovis ammon darwini*
Ovis ammon kozlovi now *Ovis ammon darwini*
Ovis ammon przewalski now *Ovis ammon darwini*

The above reclassifications now leave but one subspecies of *ammon* in the whole of Mongolia, *Ovis ammon darwini*.

[1] After Harper, *Extinct and Vanishing Mammals of the Old World*.

Classification of the Asiatic Bighorns

Ovis nivicola borealis
Ovis nivicola potanini
Ovis nivicola alleni
Ovis nivicola lydekkeri
Ovis nivicola nivicola (a form of *storcki*)

Classification of the Dall Sheep[1]

RACE

Ovis dalli dalli   Alaskan White sheep
Ovis dalli kenaiensis   Peninsula White sheep
Ovis dalli stonei   Stone or Black sheep

Previously described subspecies recently reclassified:

Ovis canadensis fannini now *Ovis dalli stonei*
Ovis canadensis liardensis now *Ovis dalli stonei*
Ovis canadensis cowani now *Ovis dalli stonei*
Ovis canadensis niger now *Ovis dalli stonei*

[1] After Ian McTaggart Cowan, "Distribution and Variation in the Native Sheep of North America," *American Midland Naturalist* (November, 1940).

Classification of the North American Bighorns[1]

RACE

The Northern Bighorns:

Ovis canadensis canadensis   Rocky Mountain Bighorn
(species type)
Ovis canadensis auduboni   Black Hills Bighorn

The Desert Bighorns:

Ovis canadensis californiana   Lava-Bed or Rimrock Bighorn
Ovis canadensis sierra   Sierra Nevada Bighorn
Ovis canadensis nelsoni   Nelson's or Desert Bighorn
Ovis canadensis mexicana   Arizona or Mexican Bighorn
Ovis canadensis texiana   Texas Bighorn
Ovis canadensis gaillardi[2]   Gaillard's Bighorn
Ovis canadensis cremnobates   Lower California Bighorn
Ovis canadensis weemsi   Weems's Bighorn

Previously described subspecies recently reclassified:
Ovis canadensis samilkamiensis now Ovis canadensis californiana
Ovis canadensis cervina now Ovis canadensis californiana
Ovis canadensis sheldoni now Ovis canadensis mexicana

[1] After Cowan, "Distribution and Variation in the Native Sheep of North America," *American Midland Naturalist* (November, 1940).

[2] While Cowan does not recognize *O. c. Texiana* and *O. c. gaillardi* as separate subspecies, believing them to be synonymous with *O. c. mexicana*, I include them here because they are still frequently referred to as such.

Comparison of an Asiatic Bighorn and an American Stone Sheep

A, The American Museum of Natural History's Kamchatka Bighorn (H. T. 24¾″); B, Chadwick's world's record Stone sheep (H.T. 31″).

THE PHOTOGRAPHS above show an interesting comparison of a fourteen-year-old Asiatic Bighorn head (A) and a ten-year-old American Stone sheep (B).

Although from different continents and of different species, they are as alike as twins, which would appear to justify their considered close relationship. In skull length they are not far apart: 10½ inches for the Kamchatka Bighorn and about 12 inches for the Stone sheep.

Originally these Asiatic Bighorns were classified as a subspecies of the American Bighorn (*Ovis canadensis*) because of their rounded horns, but lately they have been reclassified as a separate species (*Ovis nivicola*), with the several varieties being subspecies of this type.

One explanation of the close similarity in the horns of *nivicola* and the American sheep is to be found in Ian McTaggart Cowan's observation that some of the early migrants to America may have in time drifted back over the land bridge to become the present-day Asiatic Bighorns. If so, they could well have carried some of the basic horn characteristics which we now find in American forms.

Cross-Sections of Sheep Horns

SCIENTISTS DIVIDE sheep horns into two general groups, the "round"-horned and the "triangular"-horned, but because of their variable shapes and sizes it is not always easy to say which they are.

All sheep horns are basically triangular for the first three or four years of their growth, but after that they begin to bulge at the sides, becoming almost as wide as they are deep, and taking on such a variety of shapes that it is quite impossible to define them.

Confronted with this problem, I have taken many cross-sections of both types, and while these are interesting they offer no conclusive answers. A few of these sections are shown on the opposite page.

All sections were taken at the position of the five-year ring, for a just comparative reading. All sections are shown in one-quarter scale.

The orientation of each section is the same, positioned as shown in the first *Ovis vignei* arkal outline: (a), upper face of horn; (b), inner face of horn, opposing cheek; (c), outer face of horn; and (d), inner ridge of horn.

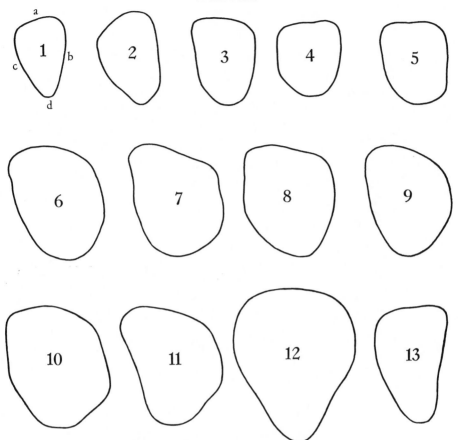

1, *Ovis vignei arkal*, seven years old; 2, *Ovis vignei vignei*, six years old; 3, *Ovis nivicola nivicola*, fourteen years old; 4, Blue sheep, fourteen years old; 5, Barbary sheep, seven years old; 6, *Ovis dalli stonei*, twelve years old; 7, *Ovis dalli dalli*, nine and one-half years old; 8, *Ovis canadensis nelsoni*, seven years old; 9, *Ovis canadensis californiana*, seven years old; 10, *Ovis canadensis canadensis*, thirteen years old; 11, *Ovis canadensis canadensis*, ten and one-half years old; 12, *Ovis ammon ammon*, ten years old; 13, *Ovis ammon poli*, ten years old.

The Sheep's Position in the Animal Kingdom

Kingdom	=	Animal
Class	=	Mammalia (mammal)
Order	=	Artiodactyla (even-hoofed animal)
Family	=	Bovidae (cattle-like animal)
Genus	=	Ovis (sheep)
Species	=	Particular kind of *Ovis*
Subspecies	=	Subdivisions of a species
Race, Form, Variety	=	Nonscientific terms for species and subspecies variations

Skull-Length Measurement as an Indication of the Relative Sizes of the Wild Sheep

BECAUSE SHOULDER-HEIGHT measurements and weights are generally so unreliable, I have resorted to a comparison of the over-all skull lengths as an indication of the relative sizes of these wild sheep.

All measurements were taken with calipers from the tip of the premaxillaries to the tip of the occipital bone at the upper rear of the skull, and all were taken of fully adult rams. I am cognizant of the variability, even among adults of any one species, and am also aware that only a large series of skulls could give a more accurate reading. Nevertheless, having so few skulls available, I offer my findings as some indication of the size relationship of the wild sheep.

In many cases only one skull was to be had, but this was far better than none. And if nothing more, we can at least see how these wild sheep grade according to size, and thereafter, by comparison, approximate the weight and shoulder-heights of a sheep when we have nothing more than its skull and horns.

Ovis vignei punjabiensis	9¾″
Ovis vignei vignei	10½″
Ovis vignei cycloceros	10½″
Ovis nivicola borealis	10½″
Ovis nivicola lydekkeri	10½″
Ovis vignei arkal	10¾″
Ovis nivicola nivicola	10¾″
Ovis dalli kenaiensis (average on five)	11″
Ovis canadensis cremnobates	11½″
Ovis canadensis weemsi (average on five)	11½″
Ovis canadensis gaillardi (average on two)	11¾″
Ovis canadensis mexicana	11⅝″
Ovis canadensis nelsoni	12″
Ovis canadensis californiana	12″
Ovis dalli stonei	12″
Ovis dalli dalli	12″
Ovis canadensis canadensis (average on six—largest, 13½″)	12½″
Ovis canadensis auduboni (twelve-year-old ram)	12½″

Ovis ammon karelini	12⅝″
Ovis ammon poli (average on seven—largest, 14″)	13⅜″
Ovis ammon littledalei (average on two—largest, 14⅛″)	13½″
Ovis ammon sairensis	13½″
Ovis ammon darwini (average on four—largest, 14⅛″)	13⅝″
Ovis ammon hodgsoni	14″
Ovis ammon ammon	15″

BIBLIOGRAPHY

1. Books

Allen, Glover M. *Extinct and Vanishing Mammals of the Western Hemisphere*. Cambridge, Mass., American Committee for International Wildlife Protection, 1942.

Andrews, Roy Chapman. *Across Mongolian Plains*. New York, D. Appleton and Company, 1921.

Burrard, Major Gerald. *Big Game Hunting in the Himalayas and Tibet*. London, Herbert Jenkins, Ltd., 1925.

Burnham, John B. *The Rim of Mystery*. London, Putnam's Sons, 1929.

Carruthers, Douglas. *Beyond the Caspian*. London, Oliver & Boyd, 1949.

———. *Unknown Mongolia*. London, Hutchinson & Company, 1913.

Clark, James L. *Trails of the Hunted*. Boston, Little Brown & Company, 1928.

Demidoff, E. (Prince San Donato). *After Wild Sheep in the Altai and Mongolia*. London, Rowland Ward, Ltd., 1900.

———. *A Shooting Trip to Kamchatka*. London, Rowland Ward, Ltd., 1904.

Dixon, J. S., and E. L. Sumner. *A Survey of Desert Bighorn in Death Valley National Monument*. N.p., California Fish and Game Commission, 1939.

Ellerman, J. R., and T. C. S. Morrison-Scott. *Checklist of Palaearctic and Indian Mammals*. London, British Museum, 1951.

Harper, Francis. *Extinct and Vanishing Mammals of the Old World*. New York, American Committee for International Wildlife Protection, 1945.

Hornaday, William T. *Campfires in the Canadian Rockies*. New York, Charles Scribner's Sons, 1907.

———. *Campfires on Desert and Lava*. New York, Charles Scribner's Sons, 1908.

Kennion, R. L. *By Mountain Lake and Plain*. London, William Blackwood & Sons, 1911.

Kinlock, Brig. Gen. Alex A. A. *Large Game Shooting; Thibet, Himalayas, Northern and Central Asia*. Calcutta, Thacker, Spink & Company, 1892.

Lydekker, Richard. *The Game Animals of India, Burma, Malaya, and Tibet*. London, Rowland Ward, Ltd., 1924.

———. *The Great and Small Game of Europe, Western and Northern Asia and America*. London, Rowland Ward, Ltd., 1901.

———. *The Great and Small Game of India, Malaya, Burma, and Tibet*. London, Rowland Ward, Ltd., 1900.

———. *Horns and Hoofs*. London, Horace Cox, 1893.

———. *The Sheep and Its Cousins*. New York, E. P. Dutton & Company, 1913.

———. *Wild Oxen, Sheep, and Goats of All Lands*. London, Rowland Ward, Ltd., 1898.

Morden, William J. *Across Asia's Snows and Deserts*. New York, G. P. Putnam's Sons, 1927.

Mumey, Nohe. *The Black Ram of Dinwoody Creek*. Denver, Range Press, 1951.

Pope, G. D. *Hunting Trails on Three Continents*. New York, Boone & Crockett Club, 1933.

Roosevelt, Theodore, Jr., and Kermit. *East of the Sun and West of the Moon*. New York, Charles Scribner's Sons, 1926.

Russo, John P. *The Desert Bighorn Sheep in Arizona*. Phoenix, State of Arizona Game and Fish Department, 1956.

Seton, Ernest T. *Lives of Game Animals*. New York, Doubleday Doran & Company, 1929.

Sheldon, Charles. *The Wilderness of the Upper Yukon*. New York, Charles Scribner's Sons, 1919.

Sowerby, Arthur de Carle. *Sport and Science on the Sino-Mongolian Frontier*. London, Andrews Melrose, Ltd., 1918.

Ward, Rowland. *Records of Big Game*. London, Rowland Ward, Ltd., 1935.

Waterer, R. R. *Protection of the Cyprus Mouflon*. London, S. Austin & Sons, 1949.

Webb, Samuel B. *Records of North American Big Game*. New York, Henry Holt & Company, 1958.

2. Articles

Cowan, Ian McTaggart. "Distribution and Variation in the Native Sheep of North America," *American Midland Naturalist* (November, 1940).

Morden, William J. "By Coolie and Caravan across Central Asia," *National Geographic*, Vol. LII, No. 4 (1927).

Nichol, A. A. "Desert Bighorn Sheep," *Arizona Wildlife Magazine* (1937).

Sowerby, Arthur de Carle. "Big Game Animals of the China-Tibetan Borderland," *China Journal*, Vol. XXVI (1937).

———. "Mammals of China, Mongolia, East Tibet, and Manchuria," *China Journal*, Vol. XXVII (1937).

Sushkin, Peter P. "The Wild Sheep of the Old World and Their Distribution," *Journal of Mammalogy*, Vol. VI (1925).

Van Gelder, Richard G. "Marco Polo's Sheep," *Natural History*, Vol. XXVIII (1928).

3. Special Reports

Allen, Glover M. *The Mammals of China and Mongolia.* Natural History of Central Asia, Vol. XI. New York, The American Museum of Natural History, 1940.

Allen, J. A. *A New Sheep from Kamchatka. Bulletin* of The American Museum of Natural History (1904).

Bailey, V. *A New Subspecies of Mountain Sheep from Western Texas and Northeastern New Mexico. Proceedings* of the Biological Society of Washington (1912).

Goldman, E. A. *A New Mountain Sheep from Lower California. Proceedings* of the Biological Society of Washington (1937).

Guillemard, F. H. H. *Remarks on Ovis nivicola. Proceedings* of the Zoological Society of London (1885).

Hornaday, William T. *Notes on the Mountain Sheep of North America, with a Description of a New Species. Fifth Annual Report* of the New York Zoological Society (1901).

Lydekker, Richard. *The Wild Sheep of the Upper Ili and Yana Valleys. Proceedings* of the Zoological Society of London (1902).

Merriam, C. Hart. *Bighorn Skull from the Plains of Western Dakota. Proceedings* of the Biological Society of Washington (1901).

Miller, Gerrit S., Jr., and Remington Kellogg. *Checklist of North American Recent Animals. Bulletin No. 205*, Smithsonian Institution (1955).

INDEX

Academy of Natural Sciences of Philadelphia: 155, 200
Adams, Mount, Washington: 190, 194
Afghanistan: vii, 27f., 30, 32, 61, 64
Afghan Urial (*Ovis vignei cycloceros*): 17, 19, 25f., 29f., 222; description of, 30; range of, 30
Akmolinsk region (Turkestan, Russian): 100
Ak Sai Plateau (Tien Shan Mountains): 84
Ala Dag Mountains, Turkey: 12
Alaska: xxv, 133, 152ff., 158
Alaskan Dall sheep (*Ovis dalli*): xix, xxv, 31, 136, 147, 152, 179, 192; color of, 155–56, 158; as a species, 156; horns of, 156, 158; size of, 156, 158; distribution of, 157 (map); relation to Asiatic Bighorns, 158; Charles Sheldon hunt, 161–67; interbreeding of, 162; integration of, 168, 169–71; classification of, 225
Alaskan White sheep (*Ovis dalli dalli*): 145, 156, 168, 225; color pattern of, xxiv; color of, xxiv; size of, 35; weight of, 156, 158; as a species, 159
Ala-tau Mountains, Russia: 95, 98
Alberta, Canada: 152, 179f., 183, 185
Alexandrovski Mountains: see Kirghiz Range
Algeria: 127f.
Allen, Glover Morrill: 130, 190
Allen, Joel Asaph: 146
Allen's Bighorn (*Ovis nivicola alleni*): 143, 224

Altai Argali: see Siberian Argali (*Ovis ammon ammon*)
Altai Mountains (Great Altai): 98, 101ff., 108f., 117, 119, 124, 129
Alta-tau Mountains: 84
Altyn Argali (*Ovis ammon dalailamae*): 223; range of, 124; description of, 124
Altyn Tagh Mountains, Sinkiang, China: 124, 223
American Bighorn: see North American Bighorn
American Museum of Natural History, New York: ix, xxviif., 50–51, 64, 74, 121, 129, 131, 139, 145, 179, 226; *poli* specimens in, 57
Ammon: see Argali (*Ovis ammon*)
Amu Darya: see Oxus River
Anadyr Range, Siberia: 144
Anadyrski Mountains: see Anadyr Range
Anatolian Urial (*Ovis ophion anatolica*): 222; range of, 12; description of, 12
Andrews, Roy Chapman: 51, 129ff., 132f.; Mongolian Argali hunt, 133–35
Aoudad sheep (*Ammotragus lervia*): habitat of, 127; description of, 127–28
Aral Sea, Russia: 24, 27
Ararat, Mount, Turkey: 13
Arctic Circle: 141, 144
Argali (*Ovis ammon*): xviii, xxv, 25, 41, 44, 46f., 98, 122, 129f., 136, 139, 180; head weight of, xx; color of, xxiv–